C000319966

FAMILY FINAN __

HOW TO MAKE YOUR MONEY GO FURTHER

Sue Thomas

A WOODHEAD-FAULKNER MONEYGUIDE

Woodhead-Faulkner · Cambridge

Published by Woodhead-Faulkner Ltd
Fitzwilliam House, 32 Trumpington Street, Cambridge CB2 1QY, England

First published 1987

British Library Cataloguing in Publication Data
Thomas, Sue
  Family finance : how to make your money
  go further—(Woodhead-Faulkner
  moneyguide).
  1. Finance, Personal—Great Britain
  I. Title
  332.024'00941   HG179

  ISBN 0-85941-420-5

Library of Congress Cataloging in Publication Data
Thomas, Sue
  Family finance : how to make your money go further / Sue Thomas.
     p.   cm.—(A Woodhead-Faulkner moneyguide)
  ISBN 0-85941-420-5 (pbk.) : $7.95
  1. Finance, Personal. 2. Family. I. Title. II. Series.
HG179.T457 1987   87-17386
332.024—dc19   CIP

Designed by Jane Norman
Typeset by Hands Fotoset, Leicester
Printed in Great Britain by Biddles Ltd, Guildford and Kings Lynn

Contents

cont.

Acknowledgements

The author wishes to express her thanks to Kathryn Deane for her assistance with the preparation of this book.

1. The ins and outs

This chapter really is the theme of the whole book – which explains where your money might come from, and where it goes to, and how to manage it successfully so that you keep your head above financial water.

In a book this size it is not, of course, possible to deal with all the aspects of this large subject in minute detail – other books in this series cover some major topics in more depth. But even so, you will find it useful to read this chapter first, before going on to the more detailed information in the later chapters: it acts as a pointer to what follows; explains the practical exercises you may need to carry out in order to take stock of your present financial position; and describes some general money points to avoid repetition throughout the rest of the book.

Because the chapter ranges over most of the material in the whole book, points which are not explained in detail here are accompanied by references to other chapters and specific pages where you will find detailed explanations.

DOING THE BOOKS

'Annual income twenty pounds, annual expenditure nineteen nineteen six, result happiness. Annual income twenty pounds, annual expenditure twenty pounds ought and six, result misery.' Micawber's advice to David Copperfield is as true today as in Dickens's time. Though money might not buy you happiness, lack of it is certainly a great cause of *un*happiness, and of the break-up of relationships. What *has* changed since Victorian times is the enormous sophistication of the money system. Your spending certainly ranges over more goods and services than Micawber could ever have dreamt about, and a significant amount probably goes on repaying money you have borrowed. Your income doesn't necessarily come from a job – it might include payments of state benefits, maintenance from a former spouse, or pensions from a grateful employer. The tax system finds ever-ingenious ways of reducing your income, often before you even get it.

It is this sophistication that makes money worries so much more likely these days. And you can't expect to tackle the system successfully – and the people who devised it all – unless you know at least the fundamentals of how it works.

The first task is to get a clear picture of where your money– or rather, that of your household as a whole – comes from and where it goes to. Only then can you know how you might get more of it in the first place, and how you can spend it more effectively in the second place. Budgeting may seem an unnecessary chore, but the secret is to devise a way of keeping tabs on your money that is quick and easy to operate. The control this gives you over your money is very satisfying, and the result may well be more freedom for you, in the shape of more money to spend on things that you want.

Money coming in

This is the easier side of budgeting, mainly because your income is likely to appear in relatively large, regular chunks. It is particularly easy if you have a full-time salaried job; you have more work to do if your income comes from a number of sources, or if it is based largely on commission, or if you are self-employed and your takings and expenses fluctuate a lot.

If you haven't bothered much about budgeting before, then you may have some hunting to do: look for payslips; maintenance payments agreements; bank or building society paying-in books or counterfoils; payment books for child benefit, pensions, etc.: records of interest paid on any savings you have; and so on. When you have collected all the information on your income, you can use it to draw up a list of what is *really* coming in week by week or month by month. Watch out for the following:

■ **Taxes.** If you are employed, your payslips will show your pay both before and after deducting tax and National Insurance, (Chapter 4, pages 30–2, 29). Certain other types of income may be paid without deduction of tax: you should work out whether and how much you will have to pay (page 22–4) and subtract it yourself, so that you don't over-estimate your income. Similarly, if you are self-employed, then treat your tax and VAT bills as expenses of the business, and make sure you deduct them *before* counting the remainder as income. On the other hand, on some payments you may be able to claim tax back (page 27, 104), in which case you should count the tax in your income.

■ **Payments that fluctuate.** Don't over-estimate what you might earn from self-employment or bonuses.

■ **Pay rises or falls.** If you are sure you are going to get a rise in pay or benefits, then you can include it in your long-term plans. But similarly, don't ignore any potential falls in income.

Money going out

It is far harder to work out what you spend than what you get. This is partly because your spending is far more piecemeal – some items daily, some weekly, some only every three months or once a year – and partly because you are likely to have even less record of where the money goes to than where it comes from. Dredge up every piece of information you can find – from your memory, cheque book stubs, the kitchen drawers, behind the mantlepiece clock, and so on – and use this checklist as a rough guide:

■ Housing – rent, mortgage, rates, repairs.

■ Fuel – electricity, gas, paraffin, coal, oil.

■ Housing – food, milk, cleaning materials, chemist, pet food.

■ Travel – bus, train, car expenses (include likely repairs, e.g. work that might be needed at the next MOT).

■ Insurances – house, your belongings, car, life, medical insurance.

■ Maintenance – if you pay any out.

■ Childminding – and babysitters.

■ Entertainment – cigarettes, drinks, going out, holidays (don't forget Christmas and birthdays), magazines and newspapers, TV and video.

■ Hobbies – gardening, DIY, sports, children's activities and pocket money.

- Loans and borrowings – credit cards, personal loans, car (if you are up to date, list only your payments, not the debt itself).
- Other expenses – an endless list: telephone, clothes, sweets, subscriptions, donations.

If you find it impossible to work out your spending from the information you have, then you must collect some more. In a diary or notebook, list *everything* you spend each day. Do this for a week or two, or longer if needs be, then go back to your budget and try again.

The information you have collected on all these expenses tells you only what has happened in the past: you must try to judge from it what you are likely to spend in the future. Though it's easier said than done, make every effort to be honest here – you fool only yourself, though you may harm other members in your household, if you under-estimate or hide any of your spending. Expect the result to shock you: almost no one believes what they are capable of spending. Work out, too, *when* you will be making the payments you have listed: more or less regularly every week or month, or not for several months?

You may realise at this stage that you have serious money problems: it may be obvious that you can't live on the money coming in, or you may have forced yourself to realise that your debts are piling up and that you cannot keep up with your repayments. For most money problems, particularly if you are in debt or are trying to live on very little money, your first port of call should be your local Citizens Advice Bureau (CAB). We mention throughout this book specific problems they can help you with, but they cover a wide range of problems, giving free, confidential, professional advice. Local CABs will be listed in a phone book, often in the front pages, and many local papers also give details of where to find them.

Where you stand

You can now make up your budget. How, and in what detail, is up to you: anything from the back of an envelope to a home computer spreadsheet will do, but a sensible middle-ground choice is a large sheet of paper you can rule off in columns (one for each month or week for as long ahead as you feel able to plan) and rows (one for each type of income and spending, plus a few more for totalling up the two groups). An example is illustrated in Fig. 1. Work in pencil, and it helps if you have a calculator.

	Oct	Nov	Dec	Jan	Feb
Balance at start of month	35.00	87.65	40.80	−26.05	−33.40
Income					
Salary	825.00	825.00	825.00	900.00	900.00
Child benefit	72.50	58.00	58.00	72.50	58.00
Monthly spending					
Mortgage	175.00	175.00	175.00	175.00	175.00
Life Insurance	24.00	24.00	24.00	24.00	24.00
Rates	49.50	49.50	49.50	49.50	49.50
Water charges	10.85	10.85	10.85	10.85	10.85
Repayments on TV and video	45.00	45.00	45.00	45.00	45.00
Car repayments	150.00	150.00	150.00	150.00	150.00
Regular spending					
Gas	80.00			110.00	
Electricity	50.00			70.00	
Telephone		65.00			80.00
House insurance					95.00
Contents insurance					
Car insurance		110.00			
Car tax			100.00		
TV licence					
Day-to-day spending					
Housekeeping	150.00	150.00	175.00	150.00	150.00
Papers	8.50	8.50	8.50	8.50	8.50
Petrol	25.00	25.00	25.00	25.00	25.00
Entertainment and sports	10.00	10.00	10.00	10.00	10.00
Miscellaneous	15.00	15.00	15.00	15.00	2.50
Irregular spending					
Car repairs and maintenance	12.00	12.00	12.00	12.00	12.00
DIY and garden	20.00	20.00			20.00
Christmas		50.00	100.00	50.00	
Clothes	10.00	10.00	50.00	75.00	
Dentist/Optician					
Holidays					
Birthdays	10.00				20.00
Total	844.85	929.85	949.85	979.85	877.35
Balance at end of month	87.65	40.80	−26.05	−33.40	47.25

Fig. 1   An example of a family budget.

When you have finished, you will be able to tell two things: are you generally spending more (or less) than you are bringing in; and are there specific weeks or months when a particular bill is going to put you in to debt? If there are problems, you should take steps now to put things right. Even if you are happy about your financial state, there's nothing wrong in checking whether you could be even happier, so read the following section anyway.

HEALTHIER FINANCES

Only when you know what is happening to your money can you move on to the next stage of trying to get more in, or spend less – in the jargon, maximising your income, and minimising your expenditure.

Maximising your income

Here are some suggestions for ways you could be getting more money:

■ Are you claiming all the social security payments you could (Chapter 6)? There is such a maze of different benefits, you may well be missing out. Don't forget possible help with housing costs (pages 72 and 93), often dealt with by your local council rather than by the Department of Health and Social Security (DHSS).

■ Is your income tax correct (Chapter 3)? You may be paying too much, particularly if your circumstances have recently changed. There are ways of claiming back tax on some payments, e.g. maintenance (page 104) or other regular payments (pages 27, 68, 116–7).

■ Have you just lost your job? You might be entitled to redundancy payments (page 38) or holiday pay (page 39).

■ Can you earn more? There may be overtime you can do, or a part-time job available (but get advice on how this might affect any social security benefits you get).

■ Can you get more interest on your savings (Chapter 14)?

Minimising your expenditure

Obviously, you could reduce your expenditure by spending less, You may well be able to tell from your budget that there are items you really needn't be buying, but the object at this stage is cutting your costs *without* reducing your standard of living. The possibilities are endless:

- Could you pay less rates (page 92)?
- Could you cut your mortgage repayments (Chapter 8)? Some types of mortgage are cheaper than others, or at least cost you less each month. But changing a mortgage can be expensive, so you need to check costs carefully.
- Can you cut insurance costs (Chapters 9 and 12)? Being fully insured is important, but you may be paying out needlessly for the wrong type of insurance. And some insurance companies charge more than others, yet don't provide a better service.
- Can you cut school fees, if your children are privately educated? There are ways (Chapter 11) other than looking for the cheapest school!
- Could you reorganise your loan repayments (Chapter 2)? The costs of borrowing money vary widely.

Spreading the load

With any luck, the result at this stage will be that you are able to live within your means, without any need for penny-pinching or more drastic measures. But you are still likely to find that there are months or weeks when a particularly large bill threatens to put you in the red – and there will certainly be expenses you can't budget for, such as expensive repairs to the car.

Planning for large bills

What you are trying to do here is to spread the costs over a period of time. Your problem may be that all the bills come in at once. Gas, electricity and phone bills for example each appear once a quarter: if you are unlucky, they will all need paying at the same time. Check whether you could reschedule two of them so that they are due one each month (you may not get far: the authorities are likely to want you to use their budget account system instead) – see below. Or perhaps you could have gas or electricity meters installed, so that you pay as you use the fuel, rather than in a big lump later.

A more serious problem is if one large bill will break the bank.

Again, see if you can break it down into smaller amounts spread over time; e.g. must you have the car resprayed at the same time as new brakes are fitted? There are special schemes for some payments: rates can be paid in monthly instalments (page 92), and there are budget accounts for gas and electricity and similar bills. These are less good if they mean you end up paying at least some of your bill in advance (which is simply enforced saving without paying you any interest). But if you can arrange for the account to include a current bill, or one that has just arrived, you will always effectively be borrowing for free. And start in late autumn, too, so that you spread the cost of the heavy winter bills over the following summer. Saving stamps, such as those you can buy for your fuel and telephone bills and television licence, certainly involve enforced savings with no interest.

If you are rich(er) in periods before these large bills are expected, then the best solution is to save up for the payment (Chapter 15) in an account where you can withdraw your money easily when the time comes; or if the date of the bill is predictable and a couple of months or more away, in a notice account which could earn you more interest (but *do* remember to give notice in time, or you could suffer penalties (page 157).

On the other hand, if the best you can manage throughout a year is just to keep solvent and you have no savings to fall back on, then the only choice is to borrow the money in some way or another (Chapter 2). Borrowing is almost always expensive, and it is very much an 'empty' expense: you are seldom any better off for having to do it. So try to avoid it if you can – perhaps by cutting your expenses beforehand so that you are able to save.

Unexpected bills

There is not much you can do about these – simply because they are unexpected. If you are fortunate enough to have some savings then you can put aside some as a special 'emergency' fund (somewhere you can get at the money instantly – page 156) which you promise yourself not to touch unless you really have to. A fund of around £500 is usually considered to be about right (but it is false economy to keep a fund for emergency expenses if it means you have to borrow to keep up with your predicted spending). Otherwise, you're back to borrowing.

Thinking about major expenses

Some expenses are just so big, it is difficult to think about them in terms of your normal day-to-day expenses. Many of these, such as a new car or house extension, you will automatically think of borrowing for (page 14), and there may simply be no other sensible way of coping with the problem. But other, slightly smaller, expenditure – such as an annual holiday – might benefit from forward planning. The rules are just the same as planning for large bills: can you spread the cost (by genuinely not borrowing), or can you meet at least some of the cost out of money you haven't spent in earlier months, or should you think about tightening your belt now, in return for the treat later?

2. Banking and borrowing

This chapter looks at ways of handling your day-to-day finances, and at the ways you can borrow when you need to.

WHERE TO PUT YOUR MONEY

Few people nowadays rely on the labelled jamjars approach to organising their money: even if you wanted to stick to cold, hard cash, most organisations with whom you have dealings will prefer to pay and receive money by cheque, or better still by some automatic means without any paper changing hands. So you will probably find yourself using some sort of financial institution – bank, post office, building society – to help you handle your income and spending.

Bank current accounts

Though the banks are being hotly pursued by other institutions, a bank current account is still likely to be your first choice: most employers are geared up to paying salaries direct into bank accounts; it is almost impossible to deal with some firms except through a bank account; loan application forms always ask you for your bank details; and there are branches of major banks almost everywhere (even if their opening hours are not always convenient). You can now do any of the following:

- Pay in money either in cash or cheques or by direct payments, e.g. of your salary by your employer.
- Keep your everyday spending money somewhere safe.
- Take out cash when you need it, either over the counter when the bank is open, or by using a machine (an automated teller machine or ATM: 'teller' is another name for a bank cashier).

- Instruct the bank to pay sums out of your account to other people, by writing a cheque.
- Make regular payments to other people, without having to remember to do so each time, either by standing order or direct debit.
- Borrow easily if your expenses temporarily exceed your income, usually in the form of an overdraft – page 17.

To help with writing cheques banks will normally give you a cheque guarantee card so you can show the person who's getting the cheque that the bank will honour it, even if you don't have enough money in your account. But this only works for cheques up to £50, which doesn't make the system all that useful.

There is a difference between standing orders and direct debits. A standing order is an instruction to the bank from *you* to pay someone else a fixed amount each month or year or whatever. A direct debit is an authorisation from you for the recipient to instruct your bank to make payments from your account; the payments may be fixed, or the recipient may have the authority to decide what they should be each time. Direct debits sound more scary, because once you've signed the authorisation, the control is in the recipient's hands. But firms operating direct debits have to be approved by the banks first, and must obey strict rules: any payments made wrongly will be refunded.

Bank charges

Do not be fooled by the advertisements for 'free' banking. It isn't free at all: ordinary bank current accounts don't pay you any interest on the money you pay in, so you are being 'charged' the interest that you could have earned on that money if you had saved it elsewhere. This could easily be £15 to £30 a year. And the banks make no charges *only* if there is money in your account. If you overdraw you will be charged for all the transactions you make through your account – sometimes for money coming in as well as going out. That seems fair enough, except that with most banks the charge is made for a whole period of, usually, three months even if you overdraw for only one day in that period.

Charges vary hugely, but expect anything from around £5 to

£15 for each period you dip into the red. If you are rarely overdrawn, and can put the situation right quickly, then a bank which has a monthly charging period is likely to be cheapest because you will pay for fewer transactions.

National Girobank

The National Girobank run by the Post Office is slightly different from other banks. You can't cash its cheques in any other bank, only at post offices. On the other hand, with 20,000 post offices, it has more branches than all the other banks put together. Its ATM is linked with building societies more than banks as it is part of the LINK network (see below).

Its charges if you overdraw are very steep, but you are charged only for the actual days on which you are overdrawn. So if you dip into the red only occasionally, and either put the situation right very quickly, or don't use the account until you can put some money in, it is likely to be the cheapest bank.

Building societies

The big bonus of a building society account is that it pays you interest on at least some of your money, so it really can be free to run, provided you do not overdraw. But building society accounts vary widely in their facilities; to be of much use they need to offer at least some of the following:

- Accepting payments direct from other people, e.g. salary from your employer.
- Bill-paying service.
- Cheque book.
- Cheque guarantee card.
- Standing orders or direct debits.
- ATMs. Many societies run ATMs connected together in two main groups – MATRIX and LINK – so you can use machines at many different societies. (The large Halifax society isn't part of the group, and runs its own ATM, as do a couple of very small societies). Because societies' ATMs are very much newer than those of the banks, they have a wider range of facilities.

The different types of account available are explained below, roughly in order of their usefulness with the most useful first.

Full cheque accounts

These work just like a bank current account. You get a cheque book with a cheque guarantee card, and probably the other bank-type facilities of standing orders or direct debits and an ATM. All your money is in a single building society account, where it earns interest.

Bank-linked accounts

Here your account is split into two. One part of your money goes into a traditional bank account, which gives you a cheque book and a guarantee card. The rest goes into a building society account, where it earns interest.

There is usually an automatic arrangement to move money from the building society to the bank, but not the other way around – so the first rule of these accounts is to make sure your payments in are made to the building society rather than to the bank; otherwise your money won't earn interest unless *you* move the money across.

There are two types of transfer. With some accounts, money is moved from the building society to the bank whenever the bank account runs low. So providing you have the funds in your building society, you won't be in danger of running up a bank overdraft. With the other type of account, you have to transfer a set amount a month. This is not so good; either you over-estimate the amount of money your bank account needs, and you have lots of money sitting idle all the time. Or you under-estimate, and your bank account becomes overdrawn – which can be expensive (possibly costing more than the interest you make on the building society account), particularly if it is a budget account (page 17) with a high interest rate.

Cheque accounts with no guarantee card

In the past, societies were not allowed to issue guarantee cards and some accounts still don't. You may not find this a grave drawback, since you can use a guarantee card only for purchases up to £50, and not at all if you are dealing by post. So you are not likely to be much worse off, particularly if you also have a credit card (see page 16) and the account includes standing orders and direct debits.

Bill paying service only

Many household bills can be paid by standing order or direct debit, and if you can set these up through a building society account, you may find you don't need a cheque book at all. (You probably need ATM facilities, and the ability to have payments made in to your account, as well.) For irregular bills, societies will write out cheques for you (see below).

Cheques to other people

All building societies will write out a cheque on their own bank account for you, withdrawing money from your account to pay for it (called a 'third party cheque'). Some will even post the cheque off to the person getting the money. Unless your money needs are very simple, it's unlikely this service on its own will be enough.

BORROWING

Borrowing is not the moral sin that it use to be and few people can resist living on 'tick' of some form or other: if nothing else, you probably have a mortgage or a credit card.

But borrowing can be a financial sin if you borrow willy-nilly, without working out how much it is costing you, and whether you can do it better elsewhere, or if you borrow without being certain you can afford the repayments – not only now, but if your income suddenly falls (e.g. you are off work sick, or are made redundant).

It is up to you to decide the second of these points; this section describes the different types of loan available, in rough order of cost with the cheapest first.

Free money

Though there may not be such a thing as a free lunch, it is possible to borrow money without paying interest.

Loans from your boss

Some employers will make you an interest-free loan as a perk of the job, often for specific purposes such as paying for an annual season ticket. That can help your overall budget (because things like travel tickets are often cheaper if you pay yearly in advance) and your month-by-month planning (because you can spread the cost at no cost to yourself – see page 6). But if the loan is large check the tax position (page 34) and find out what will happen if you leave your job: will you then have to pay interest on the loan, or will you have to repay the outstanding amount straight away (at a time when you may be least able to afford it)?

Credit cards

These can be a boon, particularly for tiding you over a bad patch because you usually don't have to pay for the things you buy until up to six weeks after you have bought them, and you don't pay any interest during this time (but see page 17 for the drawbacks).

Not as free as you think

Beware of other loans advertised as 'interest-free'. They usually aren't in practice – though you may well not be paying interest on the loan, you may find yourself paying over the odds for the goods you are buying: though carefully hidden, that's just as much a cost of borrowing as if you were paying interest. Always ask if there is a discount if you buy without taking the interest-free loan, and check the price of the goods in other places as well.

Secured loan

These are usually 'secured' (see page 73) against your home – which means that the lender can sell your home if you fail to keep up the repayments. They are therefore relatively cheap, because the lender is not taking much of a risk – but you certainly are, so make trebly sure that you can afford the repayments whatever happens.

You may have to pay extra for the setting-up of a secured loan, because the lender has to do work to find out if your security is suitable. So they are most sensible for large borrowings – say £3,000 or more.

Cheapest for a secured loan is an increase on your existing mortgage. Or you might be able to re-mortgage your house with another lender, adding on the extra money you want to borrow at the same time. (But watch out for having to pay a higher rate of interest on your whole mortgage: this would make the effective cost of the new loan much higher.) Alternatively banks (particularly for home improvements), building societies or finance houses will offer you secured loans on top of your existing mortgage. Always check up on the interest rates and any other charges.

Apart from your home, you can use other things as security, particularly a life insurance policy, the insurance company itself may make you a loan, and may only require that you pay the interest, deducting the amount you borrowed when the policy pays out.

Bank ordinary loan

This is not an overdraft on your current account, but a separate loan account. Ordinary loans can be difficult to get, mainly because banks prefer to sell you the more expensive personal loans (see below) so check that you are being offered what you want. You negotiate terms and interest rates individually with your bank, so you'll probably get the best deal if your relationship is good. When checking interest rates, watch out for 'arrangement fee' charges which may be quoted separately: if you are borrowing a small amount or for a short period, these can increase the real interest rate dramatically.

Personal loan

These are offered by banks, building societies and others – but check carefully that it's an *un*secured personal loan, rather than a secured one. You can use it for most purposes, and it is relatively easy to arrange. Watch out for how much it would cost you if you repaid the loan early – the charges can be quite high.

Credit cards

With a credit card you don't have to arrange to borrow

separately for each item you purchase. Once a month you get a statement from the credit card company showing what you have bought and provided you pay the company for all your purchases within about three weeks of the statement you don't pay any interest.

Try to use your credit card mainly for convenience in shopping and budgeting; if you do start having to pay interest the rate is high, and you have to be very disciplined not to fall into this trap. But it can be useful to tide you over a bad patch because you can use the card to borrow money; this is nearly always cheaper for a short period than overdrawing on a bank current account.

The two main credit cards are Access and Visa, available from banks and some building societies. Shops often have their own credit cards – these can be useful if they give you an interest-free period before you have to settle up, especially if the shop doesn't take the two major cards. But watch out for other types of shop 'plastic card', which may simply offer you a budget account (see below).

It is usually difficult enough with a credit card to keep out of debt. But if you do build up a credit balance most cards will not pay you interest. In fact, beware of any that do: you may find you don't get the free-loan period.

Credit sale

This is like a personal loan, except that you take it to buy specific goods, and the interest rate is often higher.

Bank overdraft

This can be very expensive. Not only do you have to pay interest on the money you borrow by going into the red but also bank charges, which can be quite high (see page 12) and which effectively push up the cost of borrowing very substantially, especially if you need to be overdrawn for only a short time.

Budget accounts

These are offered by banks and building societies. They are designed mainly to help you spread the cost of your household bills. You add up the total of your likely bills over the next year (telephone, rates, car repairs and so on) and divide by 12. You pay this sum each month into the bank account, plus something for interest, and you are allowed to write cheques for your bills as soon as they appear, whether there is enough money in the account at that time or not. If you have done your sums correctly then at the end of the year your account will be clear.

It is beautifully simple, and removes at a stroke all your budgeting worries. The catch is that it may be expensive. The interest rate when your budget account is in debt is often relatively high, and there may be other charges too. And when the account is in credit you are likely to be paid a poor rate of interest (if you get any at all).

The shop version is very similar, except that instead of working out how much you intend to spend over a year, you tell the shop how much you can afford to repay each month, and you are allowed to borrow up to 24 or 30 times that amount. Shop accounts have the same drawback as the bank accounts, plus the problem that you are more tied to shopping at one store (which is, of course what the shop wants) whether it has anything to suit you or not.

Hire purchase

This is now an old-fashioned way of buying – but the newer 'conditional sale' agreements work in similar ways. The first drawback is that they can be expensive. The second is that it is easier than with other forms of credit for the lender to take the goods back if you don't keep up with the repayments (see page 20).

Working out the cost

Most people probably compare the costs of borrowing by looking at the different repayment figures. But this is not very accurate – one shop may require a bigger deposit, another may add on arrangement fees and so on. So anyone offering you credit has, by law, to tell you the APR (annual percentage rate of interest) for the loan, and this must take into account all the charges involved in the loan. You should also be given the total cost of the deal, including the interest, any charges and the price of the goods *before* deducting any deposit.

In theory, comparing APRs should be all you need to do. But in practice it is not enough because APRs don't always take into account things like discounts you lose by not paying cash, or trade-in allowances which vary depending on the type of credit you go for. Another problem is that, despite what the law says, not all shops are very good at quoting APRs correctly.

If you are comparing the costs of borrowing the same amount for the same length of time, then looking at the total costs of the deal might be a more accurate guide to which is the best deal than an APR (even if quoted correctly).

Tax relief

If you use a loan to pay for home improvements then you may be able to claim some tax back on the interest payments, which makes the loan cheaper (see page 8). It makes no difference whether the loan is secured or unsecured – it's what it is used for that is important (unless it's a credit card or bank overdraft on which you *can't* get tax relief).

When things go wrong

When you borrow money to buy things, your rights and responsibilities are different from when you pay cash. And they may depend on the method of borrowing that you have used.

Refused credit?

There is no obligation on anyone to lend you money, and they can refuse to do so without giving you a reason. But if they do refuse it is always worth asking if they used a credit reference agency when checking you out. You have the right to be given the agencies' names and addresses, and then (for £1 each) you can ask the agencies for details of any information they hold about you: if it is wrong, they must correct it.

Changed your mind?

If you change your mind within a few days about taking a loan, even after signing an agreement, you will still have the right to cancel if you have discussed the deal face-to-face with the lender or his representative and you have signed the agreement anywhere except on the lender's premises; e.g. you talk to the

lender at the lender's premises, and then you take the
agreement home to sign.

Faulty goods?

If anything you buy is faulty, you always have some sort of
rights to force the seller to repair or replace them. If you bought
the goods on credit (and they cost more than £100) you also have
the right to force the lender to act if the seller will not or cannot.
But the loan must be linked in some way to the goods, as with
most hire purchase, conditional sales, credit agreements and
credit card purchases. A personal loan is probably not linked to
the purchase of a specific item.

Whether there is a link between the goods and the loan or not,
it is usually unwise to stop repayments if you are in dispute over
the goods: however valid your claim, you would be breaking
your contract with the lender, who would then have the right to
sue you or perhaps re-possess your goods.

Unable to keep up the repayments?

What happens depends on the type of loan. With hire purchase
or conditional sale you don't own the goods until you have
made the very last repayment. You are not allowed to sell them,
and the lender can take them back without having to give you a
penny for them, no matter how much you have paid. Your only
safeguard is that the lender has to have your permission, or has
to get a court order, if you have paid more than a third of the
total price (including the total interest due) or if the lender has to
enter your home to make the re-possession.

With other forms of credit, you do own the goods as soon as
you get them, and the lender can't just take them back. But you
can be sued in the courts, and eventually bailiffs could take any
of your possessions to help pay your debts.

More information

Shop around for credit
No credit?
Equal liability – who is responsible if things go wrong?
(All available from your local Trading Standards Department,
CAB or OFT, Government Buildings, Bromyard Avenue, Acton,
London W3 7BB)

3. Income tax

Income tax is one of the many sources of income for the Government, accounting for around a quarter of all the money it collects. The extremely complex tax system is run by the Inland Revenue who are responsible both for assessing how much tax you have to pay and for collecting it (though different departments deal with each). This chapter gives only a basic outline of the tax system – for detailed information on how to check your own tax you will need to refer to a more specialist book.

HOW INCOME TAX IS WORKED OUT

As its name suggests, income tax is a tax you pay based on your income: the higher your income, the higher your tax bill. But your pay, or profits if you are self-employed, are not all that counts as income. Most other money coming into the house – pensions, some state benefits, maintenance payments and interest you get from your savings and investments – also counts. There is a list of items that do *not* count as income, however – see Table 1, Tax facts.

You don't have to pay tax on every penny of money that counts as income. Everyone can have a certain amount of income each year before they start to pay tax, this is your 'personal tax-free allowance'. These allowances vary depending on your circumstances, e.g. a married man gets a bigger allowance than a single person and an elderly person more than a young person. The allowances are usually increased each tax year, with any changes being announced in the Chancellor's Budget.

Table 1 lists the personal allowances and the other special tax-free allowances available. (The figures apply to the 1987–88 tax year). It is important to realise how allowances work – an allowance of, for example, £3,000 doesn't mean you pay £3,000 less tax, but only that £3,000 of your income is tax-free and tax will only be payable on the rest.

Table 1   Tax facts (all figures refer to 1987–88).

Tax-free income

Social security benefits and rent and rate rebates (but not some benefits paid to people who are unemployed, pensions, widow's benefits and invalid care allowance)

Grants for improving or insulating your home. Grants or scholarships for education (unless paid by your employer)

Certain *perks* from your job (but not all – see page 32)

Pay on leaving a job Up to £25,000 in total of pay when you leave a job; e.g. redundancy pay, pay in lieu of notice

Insurance policies Some income from insurance policies, e.g. money paid by family income benefit life insurance (page 120) and the first year or so's payments from a sick pay insurance policy (page 124)

Presents or things you *inherit* (but watch out for inheritance tax – see page 128)

National Savings Cashing-in National Savings Certificates, National Savings Yearly Plan or Save-As-You-Earn

Selling things for a profit (if not a trader) – but there may be capital gains tax to pay (page 149)

Prizes or winnings from competitions, gambling, lotteries, premium bonds

Children's income is taxed as theirs, not their parents, except for income of more than £5 a year from investments which are gifts from their parents

Tax-free allowances

Main allowances
Single person's allowance For people who are single at the start of the tax year including people who are divorced or separated, women who married during the tax year and those who live together without being married   £2,425

Married man's allowance For men who are married at the start of the tax year. Men who marry during the tax year get a reduced amount of allowance   £3,795

Wife's earned income allowance For women who are married at the start of the tax year. Can only be set against the wife's earnings, not investments (page 98)   £2,425

Age allowance For the elderly, replaces the main allowances listed above. In each case you must have reached the age given by the start of the tax year
Single, 64 or over   £2,960
Single, 79 or over   £3,070
Married man's, husband
or wife 64 or over   £4,505
Married man's, husband
or wife 79 or over   £4,845

Additional allowances
Additional personal allowance For anyone unmarried and bringing up at least one child (page 100)   £1,370[1]

Widow's bereavement allowance For the tax year and the following year that a woman is widowed (page 108)
£1,370[1]

Blind person's allowance For people registered with their local authority as blind   £540[1]
(£1,080 for a married couple who are both registered)

Table 1 *cont.*

Housekeeper's allowance For a widow or widower who has someone living in who acts as housekeeper. (But you can't claim this as well as the additional personal allowance nor can you claim it if the person is a relative and someone else is claiming an allowance for him or her)   £100[1]

Son or daughter's services For anyone over 64 or disabled who has a son or daughter living in to look after them. (You can't claim this if you are a married man and your wife is under 64 unless she is disabled. Neither can you claim this at the same time as the housekeeper's or blind person's allowance – if you can get either or both of these you will save more tax. And if you are widowed you would be better off classing your son/daughter as your housekeeper as the allowance is higher)   £55[1]

Dependent relative allowance For anyone who helps to support their mother or mother-in-law who is widowed, separated or divorced or another relative who is 64 or more or disabled. The relative must live with you or you must actually pay at least £75 a year to him or her. And if their income is more than the basic retirement pension (£2,054) you will lose £1 of the allowance for each £1 their income is over this limit   £100[1,2]

Claimable outgoings

Interest on loans and mortgages you take out to buy or improve your home (pages 73, 81)

Pension contributions If you are in a job, you will automatically get tax relief on your contributions to your employer's pension scheme, as your employer deducts the contributions from your pay before working out how much tax to deduct. If you pay into a personal pension you get basic-rate tax relief by making reduced payments, as with most mortgages. If you are self-employed you have to include your pension payments on your business accounts and your taxable profit will be reduced by the payments you have made

Maintenance you have to pay after separation or divorce (page 104). Unless the payments are below certain limits and count as 'small maintenance payments' you usually give yourself basic-rate tax relief by subtracting the equivalent of basic rate before handing the money over.

So if you have to pay £200 you would deduct £54 – 27% of £200. If you are a higher rate tax payer you will get the extra relief either through the PAYE system or by getting a smaller tax bill

Payments you make under covenant (page 27). Here you give yourself basic-rate tax relief by subtracting the equivalent of basic-rate tax before making the payments. You can't get relief at higher than basic rate if the covenant is to a person – your student son or daughter, for example. But if the covenant is to a charity you can get higher-rate tax relief – show the covenant payments on your tax return and you will get the extra relief either through an adjustment in your PAYE code or by getting a smaller tax bill

Expenses in your job but only if they are a necessary part of your job . You have to show these payments on your tax return (or let the Inland Revenue know about them). You will get tax relief by getting a higher PAYE code

cont.

---

[1] Paid in addition to a main personal allowance
[2] £145 if you are a single woman or married woman who has chosen to have her earnings taxed separately from those of her husband (page 98)

Table 1 *cont.*

Separate taxation of wife's earnings

Married couples will pay less tax this way (page 98) if the joint income is at least £26,870 and the less well-off partner has at least £6,545 (*earned* income only if it's the wife's). As combined earnings increase, the minimum income for the less well-off partner reduces, but it never drops below £4,916. If you think you might benefit, ask your tax office for details.

Age allowance trap

If you are over 64 and your income is more than £9,800 you will lose £2 of your age allowance for every £3 by which your income is more than £9,800 (page 67). It will never be reduced below the single person's or married man's allowance.

You will get no benefit from age allowance if your income is:

- £10,603 if you are single aged 64 to 79 before the start of the tax year
- £10,768 if you are single aged 79 or more
- £11,120 if you are married and either partner is 64 to 79 before the start of the tax year
- £11,375 if you are married and either partner is 79 or more

For tips on how to avoid this trap see page 68.

Tax rates

Tax rate	Paid on taxable income from	to
27%	£1	£17,900
40%	£17,901	£20,400
45%	£20,401	£25,400
50%	£25,401	£33,300
55%	£33,301	£41,200
60%	£41,201	

Tax years

Tax years are not the same as calendar years. They run from 6 April one year to the 5 April the following year. So the 1987–88 tax year runs from 6 April 1987 to 5 April 1988.

Finally you don't have to pay any tax on income which you spend on certain things. In the jargon these are known as 'outgoings' and you get 'tax relief' on them. For example, if you pay into a pension scheme you get tax relief on your contributions. So if you paid £1,000 into a pension plan in a year, you would pay tax on £1,000 less of your income. There are various outgoings you can claim and the way you get your tax relief varies from one to the other. See Table 1 for details.

The result after you have worked out what counts as your 'income', and deducted your allowances and outgoings from it, is called your 'taxable income'. If your taxable income is greater than zero, you will have to pay a proportion of it in tax. How much you will pay depends on the tax rates currently in force. These give you the percentage of your taxable income you have to pay in tax (they are sometimes shown as 'pence in the £'). For example, if your taxable income is £7,000 and income tax is charged at 25p in the £ (25%) your tax bill will be £7,000 × 25% = £1,750.

The proportion increases as your income increases. For example, in the 1987/88 tax year (see Table 1 for an explanation of tax years), the lowest rate of tax is 27% or 27p in the £; most people who have to pay tax pay only this basic rate. People whose taxable income is more than £17,900 have to pay higher rates, ranging from 40% to 60%. See Table 1 for details.

DEALING WITH THE INLAND REVENUE

The first rule is that you have to tell the Inland Revenue about any taxable income you get; do not wait to be asked or you may be running up a large bill which you may not be given time to pay. Equally if your circumstances change – for instance you get married or divorced, or reach 64 – let the Inland Revenue know straight away so that there is no delay in your being given your correct tax-free allowances. Tax returns (forms the Inland Revenue send out to get full details of your financial affairs and circumstances) are not sent to all taxpayers each year. If you are employed and have relatively straightforward tax affairs you may not get a tax return for several years. So be vigilant about your affairs – if you get income which you don't tell the Inland Revenue about you could be fined up to £100.

The second rule is that if you get any correspondence from the Inland Revenue, send any reply within the time limit given. For example, if the Inland Revenue make an assessment of your income and send a tax bill with it you have 30 days in which to appeal against the assessment and ask for the bill to be postponed. If you do not reply in this time you will be able to get any mistakes put right only if you had a good reason for not replying in time.

How income tax is collected

There are two main ways in which tax is collected:

■ The person paying you the money may have to deduct tax and pay it directly to the Inland Revenue. This happens with certain types of income from investments, and if you work for an employer or get an occupational pension, tax may be deducted under the PAYE (Pay As You Earn) system – see Chapter 4 for details of PAYE.

■ By sending you a tax demand if you are self-employed, or have a lot of investment income, or very complicated tax affairs.

Tax rebates

If you think you have paid too much tax in a year you can claim back the excess. For example, if you give up a job to have a baby part way through the tax year and will not be returning until the following tax year you will have paid too much tax. Or you might discover that you have not been getting the right allowances for a couple of years. You can claim rebates for up to six years after you paid the tax.

If you think you should be getting a rebate, just write to your tax office, explaining what you think you should get and why. (If you are unemployed and claiming benefits you will not get any rebate you are due until after the end of the tax year or until you get another job if this is sooner).

Help

If you want to find out more about tax, or want to check that you are paying the correct amount or want to sort out problems there is a lot you can do yourself.

> **Step 1** Get any appropriate Inland Revenue leaflets. They vary from providing only basic information through to being extremely full statements of how the Inland Revenue interpret the tax laws. There are basic leaflets to explain the PAYE system, the tax situation on separation and divorce, on marriage, for one-parent families and so on. Ask your local tax office for leaflets.

> **Step 2** Consult the *Which? Tax Saving Guide* published each March or the *Which? Book of Tax*. They are two of the clearest guides to the tax system, though you will find many others in your local bookshop.

> **Step 3** Consult your tax office. They should be able to help clear up any straightforward problems such as with PAYE. (If you write, it could take some time to get a reply, so phone or call instead.)

> **Step 4** If your affairs are really complex, or if you are self-employed, an accountant or solicitor may be able to help you sort things out. But you need someone used to dealing with similar problems, so see if a friend can recommend anyone.

SAVING TAX BY USING COVENANTS

A covenant is a binding agreement by which you agree to make a series of payments to another person. You then get tax relief on the payments and the recipient pays any tax that is due. But if the recipient does not have enough income to owe any tax, neither of you will have to pay any. So a covenant is a tax-efficient way of agreeing to give money to someone who has little or no taxable income. To get the tax relief:

- neither you nor your husband or wife must benefit from the payments;
- if you want money to go to your own child he or she must be 18 or more (or married);
- the covenant must be intended to last for more than six years (more than three years if it is to a charity) though once it is set up it can be ended earlier than this if both you and the recipient agree.

How a covenant works

Say you decide you want to give £500 a year to your grand-daughter and draw up a deed of covenant. Before handing over the £500 you give yourself basic-rate tax relief by deducting 27% of £500 so your grand-daughter gets £365. Her income (including the 'gross' amount you have covenanted, i.e. £500) is well below her personal allowance assuming she has little other income, so she can claim back from the Inland Revenue the £135 tax you deducted. For a cost of only £365 to you, your grand-daughter gets £500.

You can usually get tax relief only at the basic rate. But if the covenant is made to a registered charity you can get relief at your highest rate of tax, though you still deduct only basic-rate tax before making your payments, and claim back the rest of the tax relief when you fill in your tax return.

To ensure that the person you are making payments to gets the tax you have deducted you should fill in a form (R 185AP) each year, give it to the recipient to complete and then he or she sends it to their tax office.

To get tax relief the covenant must be drawn up correctly – there are rules which must be followed. If you are making a covenant to a student son or daughter the Inland Revenue produce a standard form; ask your tax office for a copy. And most charities will have standard forms too. If you want to covenant money to someone else, get advice from the tax office on the wording.

4. Money and your job

With any job – whether it is your first or your umpteenth, whether it is part-time or full-time – it's not just the basic pay that is important. You need to know all sorts of other things: what all the figures on your payslip mean, how much your perks are worth, what happens if you are off sick or leave to have a baby and what other rights you have. Many people find it hard to make ends meet even if they are in work, so this chapter also includes information on the benefits you might be able to claim.

WHAT YOUR PAYSLIP TELLS YOU

No matter where you work or how you are paid you have the right to get a pay statement setting out various things about your pay:

- Gross pay – your total pay before any deductions are made, including any overtime, holiday pay or bonuses.
- What deductions are made from your pay, e.g. National Insurance, tax, pension contributions, trade union subscriptions.
- Net pay – your actual take-home pay after all deductions have been made.

If you do not get a detailed pay statement and your employer will not provide one, you can complain to an independent industrial tribunal.

National Insurance contributions

If your gross pay is more than a certain amount in any week you have to pay National Insurance contributions, which will provide you with state help such as unemployment benefit and sickness pay if you need them. You do not have to pay contributions if you are a woman aged 60 or more or a man 65 or more. For the tax year starting 6 April 1987 the lower earnings limit is £39 a week. Once you earn at least this much you will pay contributions on the whole of your earnings up to an upper earnings limit which is £295 a week in 1987–88. How much you pay depends on your earnings and what sort of pension scheme you are contributing to. And some married or divorced women pay reduced rates (see page 132). If you work for more than one employer you have to pay contributions on your earnings from each job, though there are limits to how much you have to pay in total.

Income tax

One of the deductions (probably the largest) shown on your payslip will be for tax. The system used for collecting tax on your earnings is called Pay As You Earn (PAYE) and, unless you become self-employed or earn too little to have to pay tax, you will pay tax this way all through your working life (and beyond if you get a pension from your job). The PAYE system may also be used to collect tax due on other income besides your earnings, such as your state retirement pension or regular freelance earnings.

Each year the tax office works out your PAYE code which your employer uses to calculate the right amount of tax to deduct from your pay. Broadly speaking each month (or week) 1/12 (or 1/52) of the amount of tax you will owe over the whole year is deducted from your pay before you get it. When your code is calculated your tax office will send you a Notice of Coding which shows what tax-free allowances you get and what outgoings are included (see Table 1), These are added together and then any extra income which is being taxed under PAYE is deducted.

There can be other information included in your Notice of Coding. If you have under-paid tax in previous years, or owe extra higher-rate tax on investment income which has had only basic-rate tax deducted before you get it, this may be shown as another deduction on your Notice. Or, if you pay tax at more than basic rate, you may be due extra tax relief on maintenance payments, mortgage interest or on covenanted payments to charities.

The amount left at the end is what you can earn throughout the tax year without paying any tax. This is converted to your PAYE tax code by removing the last figure and adding a letter. The letter gives your employer information on what tax allowance you claim, so that if the personal allowances are altered your PAYE code can be adjusted without having to wait for the tax office to issue a new Notice of Coding. This speeds things up a lot and means that within a month or so of the new tax year your code can be changed to reflect any higher tax-free allowances announced in the Budget. The letters used are as follows:

L if you get the single person's or wife's earned income allowance.

H if you get the married man's allowance or single person's plus additional personal allowance.

P if you get the full age allowance for a single person.

V if you get the full age allowance for a married couple.

T can mean either that you don't want your employer to know what allowance you get or that you are getting a reduced amount of age allowance (see page 67). Your employer will have to wait for a new tax code from your tax office before putting any Budget changes into effect.

F means that your pay (or occupational pension) has to be taxed at a higher-than-normal rate in order to collect the tax due on other income at the same time (see page 69) for an example.

BR or D codes are usually given for your earnings from a second job when all your allowances are being given against your pay in your first job.

Always check your Notice of Coding carefully. Make sure that all the allowances you are claiming are on it and that any estimates for income not taxed when you get it are reasonable. If not, let your tax office know straight away. Do the same if your circumstances change during the tax year – for example if you get married or separate. Then your employer will be given details of your new code so that you won't be paying too much (or too little) tax.

Pension contributions

Not all firms run their own pension schemes. But those that do usually ask employees to pay a certain percentage of their earnings into the scheme if they want to be members. If your employer's pension scheme is either approved by the Inland Revenue or is a statutory scheme (if you are a civil servant or employee of a local authority or nationalised industry) you will not pay tax on your contributions (see page 135) so these will be deducted from your pay before your tax is worked out. The same will apply to contributions you make to one of the new minimum personal pension plans instead of the government's pension scheme (see page 134).

More information

Itemised pay statement
(Employment Legislation Booklet 8, available from your local Department of Employment or CAB)
NI40 National Insurance guide for employees
NI208 National Insurance contribution rates
NP28 More than one job?
(All available from your local DHSS)
IR34 Income Tax – PAYE
(Available from your local tax office)

PERKS

Your pay may not be the only thing you get for working. You may also get perks (sometimes known as fringe benefits) such as a company car, season ticket loan or luncheon vouchers. All of these are worth something to you – an interest-free season ticket loan saves you having to borrow money, a subsidised canteen means you can have cheap meals when at work – and so you have to pay tax on most fringe benefits. But not all: the most common tax-free fringe benefits include the following:

- Special clothes needed for your work, e.g. overalls.
- Staff outings.
- Free or cheap food and drinks.
- Free life insurance.

- Luncheon vouchers (up to 15p for each working day).
- Free sport and social facilities.
- The cost of free sick pay insurance.
- Discounts on the firm's own products or services.

Other perks are taxable, and the Inland Revenue decides how much pay the perk is worth and taxes you on that amount. Sometimes the value of the perk is what your employer has had to pay for it. For instance if you're given a voucher to buy a season ticket or to buy clothes you'll be taxed on what it cost your employer – not on the value of what the voucher will buy.

But with a great many perks what tax you pay (or indeed whether you will pay anything at all) depends on how much you earn: once the total of your pay plus the taxable value of your perks comes to more than a certain amount (£8,500 in the 1987–88 tax year) you count as 'higher-paid' and more perks will be taxed. For instance, if your employer provides you with private patients' insurance (see page 125) or a crèche for children, you pay tax based on what the perks costs your employer (less anything you pay towards the perk) if you are higher-paid, but you won't pay any tax if you do not count as higher-paid.

The rules for cars and interest-free or cheap-interest loans are a little more complicated.

Cars

A company car is always a popular perk and tends to be something of a status symbol. For most people it is worth far more then the tax they have to pay (and it is an even more valuable perk if you do not count as higher-paid as then you will not pay any tax at all on it).

The taxable value of a company car depends on its age, the engine size, how much it cost when it was new, and how many miles you cover on business in the year. For example, a car less than four years old, costing less than £19,250 when new and with an engine size of 1400cc or less has a taxable value of £525 in the 1987–88 tax year (£580 in the 1988–89 tax year).

If you get free petrol for private use this also has a taxable value, which depends only on the engine size of the car, not on how much petrol you get. For a car with an engine capacity of 1400cc or less the taxable value of petrol for private use is £480 in the 1987–88 and 1988–89 tax years.

Cheap loans

If your employer gives you a loan which qualifies for tax relief (e.g. a cheap mortgage – see page 81) you will not have to pay any tax on the benefit you get from it no matter how much you are paid. But if the loan doesn't qualify for tax relief – for instance if it is for a season ticket – its taxable value is the difference between the interest you pay (if any) and what you would pay if you were charged the offical rate of interest (12% for the 1987–88 tax year). If this value doesn't bring you into the higher-paid bracket you won't pay any tax on a cheap loan. And if the taxable value of your loan (or loans) is £200 or less you won't pay any tax even if you are higher-paid.

YOUR RIGHTS AT WORK

Pay and perks are not the only aspects of a job that affect your finances. Getting six weeks' paid holiday a year is likely to be more valuable to you than four weeks'. And knowing that you will get full pay if you are ill for a few weeks is reassuring.

Your contract

The law says that once you have been in a job for more than 13 weeks (as long as you work for more than 16 hours a week) you must be given a statement which sets out the main terms and conditions of your employment including the following:

- How much you are paid, including details of any overtime pay.
- How often you are paid and when.
- Conditions about hours of work.
- Details about how much holiday you get.
- Details about what sickness pay you will get.
- Disciplinary procedures.

This is all many people get in the way of a written 'contract' for their job and is all the law entitles you to. But if you are in dispute with your employer, bear in mind that a contract can include anything you agree with your boss about your conditions or work, even if it is not in writing. And it can even include behaviour which has never been agreed, but which has simply always happened (called 'custom and practice').

Pay if you are ill

If you are unable to go to work because of illness it is unlikely that your pay will stop completely. There are state benefits which you may get – the main one is statutory sick pay (SSP) and many employers will top up your pay. You can also take out insurance to help pay the bills if you are ill (see page 123).

It is important to find out what your contract says about sick pay. Check that you know about the following points:

- How much you will get and how long it will be paid for.
- When it starts. Do you have to be off work for a few days without pay before you get anything? (Some firms do this to try to discourage their employees from taking odd days off when they're just feeling a little under the weather.)
- When you have to notify your employer that you are ill. Some firms will want a sick note signed by your doctor straight away (though they can't make this a condition of giving you your SSP for the first week); others will simply accept your word or a certificate you've signed yourself (SC1 from your doctor's surgery or DHSS offices) for the first week you're off work.

Statutory sick pay

The rules for this are quite complicated but broadly you will get it unless:

- you are over pension age (60 for a women, 65 for a man);
- you earn so little that you don't have to pay National Insurance contributions (less than £39 a week in the 1987–88 tax year);
- you have already had 28 weeks of SSP in the same spell of illness from the same employer;
- you have been getting invalidity pension, sickness benefit or maternity allowance within the last eight weeks.

If you are not in one of these excluded groups your employer will start paying you SSP once you have been off work for more than three days. How much you get depends on your normal weekly earnings before deductions. In the 1987–88 tax year you will get £47.20 a week if your average weekly earnings were £76.50 or more or £32.85 if they were between £39.00 and £76.49.

You pay tax and National Insurance on your SSP in the same way as you do on your wages. If you are off work for more than 28 weeks you'll stop getting SSP and will have to claim sickness benefit or invalidity benefit from the DHSS (see page 56).

Employer's sick pay

Not all employers pay sick pay on top of SSP, and they do not have to. Even if they do, you will not get SSP as well as your normal wages. Instead the SSP is topped up to, say, all or half your usual pay. And there are usually time limits, for instance one month on full pay followed by two months on half pay. After that you get just SSP.

If you can't manage on what you get from your employer when you are off work sick you may be able to get help from the DHSS; see Chapter 6.

Maternity rights

No longer do you have to give up your job a few weeks before your baby is due and simply hope that you will be able to find another post afterwards. Many working women have the right to have time off work for pre-natal care, to statutory maternity pay (SMP) when they stop working to have a baby, and to return to their job after the baby is born. For other help that may be available see Chapter 11.

Statutory maternity pay

When you give up work to have a baby your employer will have to pay you SMP for 18 weeks if:

- you have been working for him or her for at least six months at the end of the fifteenth week before your baby is due;
- you normally earn enough to pay National Insurance contributions;
- you stop work any-time between the eleventh and the sixth weeks before the week in which your baby is due.

If you meet all these conditions you will get £32.85 (the lower rate) a week in the 1987–88 tax year. And if you have been working for the same employer for 16 hours a week or more for the last two years your SMP will be made up to 9/10ths of your average weekly pay for the first six weeks in which you claim SMP. (If you work less than sixteen hours but more than eight hours a week you need to have been with the same employer for five years or more before being able to claim this).

You have to pay tax and National Insurance on your SMP in the same way as you do on your wages. But while you get the lower rate you won't be earning enough to pay National Insurance and may not have to pay tax either. In fact, because of the way the PAYE tax system works you may get a tax rebate in each pay packet.

If you have been working for your employer for less than six months you may be able to claim maternity allowance from the DHSS instead of SMP. If you have paid enough National Insurance contributions you will get £30.05 a week (tax-free) for up to 18 weeks.

Returning to your job

All working women who have been with the same employer for at least two years at the start of the eleventh week before the week in which the baby is due have the right to return to their previous job after the birth of a baby. (If you work between eight and sixteen hours a week you need to have been with the firm for at least five years to have this right.) But you must let your employer know that you are going to be taking maternity leave at least three weeks before you intend to start it and say that you want to return to your job after the baby is born. Even if you think that you will want to stay at home it is wise to say you want to return to work – you may change your mind when you have been at home a few months, or you may find your circumstances have changed so that you need to work.

After the baby is born you have to go back to work within 29 weeks; you must give your employer at least three weeks' warning, in writing, of when you intend to go back to work. (If your employer writes to you before this asking if you intend to return you must confirm in writing, within 14 days of getting the letter, that you still want to go back, though at this stage you do not have to give a date.) Of course at any time you can decide not to go back but it is wisest not to make a final decision until your 29 weeks are up.

Leaving work

Whatever the reason you have for leaving a job, you may be entitled to extra pay. This section looks at your rights (and responsibilities) whether you leave voluntarily or are sacked. If you do not have another job to go to straight away, read also Chapter 6.

Redundancy

The situation of firms closing down completely or cutting their workforce to cut costs and improve efficiency is a common feature of life in the 1980s. Many employees are entitled to compensation for the loss of their jobs and what you get is laid down by law (although there is nothing to stop your firm offering a higher amount). How much you get under the state scheme depends on the following:

- How long you have been with the firm. To get anything you have to have been there for at least two years.
- How much you earn (there is a limit that can count when working out redundancy pay: £158 from April 1987).
- How old you are (if you are a woman aged 60 or more or a man of 65 or more you are not entitled to any redundancy pay – though women should see 'Retirement ages' below).

   Your redundancy pay will be the total of:

- half a week's pay for each complete year you were with the firm between the ages of 18 and 21,
- one week's pay for each complete year between the ages of 22 and 40, and
- one-and-a-half week's pay for each complete year after the age of 41.

Pay in lieu of notice

By law an employer has to give you at least a certain minimum period of notice if he or she wants you to leave your job. If you work at least 16 hours a week, once you have been in a job for a month you must be given one week's notice and if you have been employed for two years or more you must be given one week's notice for each complete year of employment up to a maximum of 12 weeks. (These are the minimum figures – your contract may say that you have to be given longer periods of notice, but you cannot be given less.)

Unless you are sacked on the spot for 'gross misconduct' – for instance for stealing or for assaulting another employee – you have the right to get pay instead of this notice. If you don't you can sue in the county court for wrongful dismissal.

As an employee you have to give your employer at least one week's notice if you want to leave your job. This minimum does not increase with length of service. But your contract may require you to give longer notice. Theoretically your employer could sue you if you do not give enough notice; in practice this is unlikely to happen.

Holiday pay

When you leave a job you may find that you have not taken all the holidays you are allowed. Whether or not you will get pay instead depends very much on the terms of your contract.

Unfairly sacked

If you are sacked, or if you leave your job because you feel you have been forced to, as long as you have been employed by the firm for two years or more you have the right to complain to an industrial tribunal. The result of this can be that you get your job back (or another post in the same firm) although most people opt for compensation. This is paid in two parts. The first is calculated in a similar way to redundancy pay (see above); the other depends on how much you actually lose by being out of a job, i.e. it's what you would have earned less any money you have received. If you want to take your employer to an industrial tribunal it is important to get help, e.g. from your union or from a Citizens Advice Bureau – but it is most important that you make your application within three months of your last day at work.

Retirement ages

The traditional age for retiring from work is 60 for women and 65 for men. At these ages you can start drawing your state pension. There is nothing to stop you working after this age and it can increase your state pension and pension from your job considerably. But you do lose lots of your employment rights – for example, you cannot claim unfair dismissal or get redundancy pay under the state scheme. However, lots of employers do not allow employees to stay on after they reach state pension age. This means that women are forced to retire five years earlier than men.

But there are changes on the way. European Community law is very keen on women and men being treated equally and fairly. Already the courts in this country have decided that women who work for public sector employers – civil service, local government, health authorities and so on – can stay in their jobs until they are 65. They also retain the rights to claim unfair dismissal, redundancy pay and so on. And by late 1987 a law should be in force which gives all women the right to work until they are 65 if they want to.

More information

Written statement of main terms and conditions of employment
Employment rights for the expectant mother
Rights on termination of employment
Procedure for handling redundancies
Unfairly dismissed?
(All available from your local Job Centre or CAB)
FB28 Sick or disabled?
FB15 Injured at work
FB8 Babies and benefits
NI17A Maternity benefits
(All available from your local DHSS or CAB)

LOW PAID?

If you do not earn much – either because you are in a low-paid job or because you can work only part-time – it may be possible to increase your income by claiming state help such as family income supplement or income support, or housing benefit.

Families with children

Until 5 April 1988 you may be able to claim family income

supplement (FIS) as long as you (or your partner) work at least 30 hours a week (a single parent has to be working at least 24 hours). The amount you get depends on how much you earn, how many children you have and how old they are. As an example, a couple (or single parent) earning £90 before deductions with two children under 11 could get £11.30 a week FIS. The family would also get free school meals, free dental treatment and prescriptions, vouchers to help with the cost of spectacles and possibly a maternity payment of £80 (see page 110). You may also get extra if you have to pay for a funeral (see page 108).

From April 1988 'family credit' replaces FIS. You will be able to claim this if you (or your partner) work at least 24 hours a week. How much you get will depend on how much you earn, your savings, how many children you have and how old they are. Family credit does not give automatic entitlement to free school meals but the other welfare benefits are still available.

If you (or your partner) do not work enough hours to get this help you may be able to claim supplementary benefit or income support instead (see page 61).

Help with housing costs

If you pay rent and/or rates you may be able to get help from your local council under the housing benefit scheme. Whether you get help and how much you get depends on your family circumstances – how many children you have, their ages, whether any grown-up children or other relatives live with you, how much you pay in rent and rates, what income you have and how much you have in savings. To get an idea of whether you might be able to get help see page 72.

More information

FIS1 Family income supplement
FB2 Which benefit?
FB27 Bringing up children
(All available from your local DHSS or CAB)

5. Working for yourself

Working for yourself can include anything from doing a few hours teaching a week to running a 1,000-acre farm or a factory employing large numbers of workers. There is certainly a greater chance of making money, and enjoying the other trappings of success by running your own show than by working for someone else. But you will need to know more than you ever thought possible on a wide range of subjects, from how to set up a business (and even, should you?) to how to deal with income tax, VAT, insurance and employees.

HOW TO SET UP IN BUSINESS

Every year many people set themselves up in business for the first time but many of them will not last for more than a couple of years. You will have a better chance of success if you know what is in store before you start so that at least you get off on the right foot.

Should you run a business?

To ensure that you have a good chance of being successful there are two rules:

- Be certain that you have the qualities and the drive to succeed.
- Do your homework to make sure your project has a chance of success and make sure you start with enough cash.

Running your own business gives you independence and control – you decide what work you want to do and when, you choose the people you employ, you decide when you go on holiday. You may be able to work from home. But the other side of the coin is having less financial security – your income may be irregular and your entitlements to state benefits lower, and if you want benefits like sick pay, holidays and pensions you have to pay for them yourself. You will probably find yourself working long hours and it may be more difficult to leave work problems behind at the end of the day. And of course, there will be lots of paperwork.

Ask yourself the following questions. The more you are able to answer 'yes', the better:

- Are you prepared to work very long hours?
- Do you have the support of your family?
- Can you make decisions and accept responsibility for them?
- Can you work under stress?
- Can you cope with paperwork?
- Are you willing to seek advice?
- Can you cope with taking financial risks?
- Can you cope with working on your own without colleagues or a boss to fall back on?
- Are you absolutely determined to succeed?

You might have the business drive, and you might also have a brilliant idea that you are convinced will make your fortune. But don't rush in – someone else may already be providing the product or the service or there simply may not be a market for it.

Find out as much as you can about the field you plan to enter. Read the trade journals, do research in your local library, find out about your competition and find out what is already available. Make a list of who your customers are likely to be – do not ignore contacts you have made through your own employment (though watch out for any conditions in a contract which might restrict you working in similar fields – get advice from a solicitor if there is such a clause).

Think why customers will want to buy from you rather than from other people. Will your product or service be different or can you ensure that it is an improvement on what is available at the moment? Work out your costs very carefully: don't be tempted to assume you can sell your product or service at a lower cost than your rivals. How much will you need to sell to make your business viable?

How much is starting your business going to cost and how

much will it cost to run? You need to think about equipment –
basic equipment such as a typewriter or word-processor for an
office-based business, or tools to enable you to make products or
offer the service you intend to sell. Will you buy or rent such
equipment? What about telephones? What do you need to buy
in the way of materials? Will you need to advertise your
business?

How much are you going to charge for your service or your
product? Remember to charge for your time (and that of any
employees) as well as passing on the cost of raw materials, the
phone bill, stationery costs, using the car on business, advertising and the costs of setting up. And don't forget that you
need to make a profit – if you sell too cheaply you will end up
with bills you can't pay and will fail.

Types of business

There are three main ways of going into business: on your own
as a sole trader, in a partnership with one or more other people,
or by forming a limited company. It is also possible to set up a
business as a co-operative, or to buy a franchise.

Sole trader

Running a business as a sole trader is simple – there are no legal
formalities to go through (though you should tell the Inland
Revenue and the DHSS, and certain kinds of business need a
licence), and you will not need to have your accounts audited.
The business is all yours – but so are all its debts, and in the last
resort your possessions (including your home) could be sold to
pay your debts. But many small businesses are run quite
smoothly by a sole trader.

Partnership

A partnership is similar in that there are no legal formalities. But
it is wise to draw up a proper partnership agreement between
the partners so that everyone knows the exact terms under
which the partnership is operating. Get advice from a solicitor to
do this. Profits of a partnership are shared by the partners (often
in proportion to the money put in but the terms should be
clearly stated in the agreement) but each partner is responsible

for the whole debts of the partnership. So be careful who you choose as your partner or partners – you each need to be dedicated to whatever you are doing and agree on where the business is heading. The positive side is that you can find partners whose skills and experience are strong in areas where you are weak. For example if you intend to sell plants and have all the horticultural expertise you could choose a partner who is good at marketing and selling.

Limited company

A limited company has a legal existence all of it its own separate from the people who run it. This is where the main advantage lies, as if the company runs into financial problems your liability for debts will be limited to the amount you paid for your shares. (However, some lenders and suppliers may insist on personal guarantees that they will be paid, and you will have to pay on any guarantees you have undertaken.) There is a fair amount of legal work and cost involved in setting up and running a limited company: it must be registered with the Companies Registration Office, and accounts have to be audited and filed each year. Directors are paid employees of the company but can also benefit from any dividends the company pays. You certainly need legal advice if you are thinking of setting up a limited company.

Co-operative

A co-operative is a different sort of business where everyone involved shares the responsibility for decisions and the rewards. A co-operative may be a limited company or have limited liability by being registered under the Industrial and Provident Societies Acts.

Franchise

Buying a franchise enables you to sell the franchising company's products or services using its name – Wimpy, Kentucky Fried Chicken, Dyno-Rod are all franchised businesses. But although you get some help, you own the business and will have to bear any losses. You can trade as a sole trader, as a partnership or as a company.

Sources of advice

You may need advice at any stage of setting up and running your business. There are all sorts of groups, organisations and individuals able to offer advice, A few sources of general help and advice are described below – if you need more specific information, they will tell you where to go.

Local enterprise agency and Small Firms Service

Advisers can take you through all the basic steps of setting up in business, as well as advising on premises, getting finance, formulating your business plan, how to deal with accounts and so on. Once you have had several advice sessions you may have to pay a fee for more help. Your local Job Centre or CAB will be able to tell you if there is a local enterprise agency and you can get in touch with the Small Firms Service by phoning 'Freephone Enterprise'.

Professional services

An accountant can help you with your financial decisions, give advice on keeping tax and other accounts records, supply VAT information and help you decide what legal form your business should take. If you need to borrow money to start off your business you will need an accountant's help to formulate your business plan. A solicitor can advise on renting premises, setting up a partnership or a company, contracts and so on. Ask other local businesses for advice on which solicitor or accountant to go to – you need someone used to small businesses. A bank manager's support can be invaluable if you need to borrow money. If you have a good proposal but your bank manager is not interested, shop around.

Your business plan

All your homework and research will help you to formulate a business plan. Putting your plan on paper will help show up flaws in your ideas, and give you something to discuss with other people whom you may not want to approach for advice or money. Even if you are starting out in a very small way a business plan is important as it will help you to get your ideas organised. Your plan could include the following:

- What your business will provide.
- What your experience (and that of any partners) and knowledge is of the field in which you intend to trade.
- What evidence you have that there is a market for your idea and how you intend to sell it. Why are you different from your competitors?
- What you need in the way of resources – employees, equipment, premises, and money.
- How you have costed what you will be providing and how much it will cost your customers.
- How much money you need and how much you can provide without borrowing.
- When you expect to be showing a profit.
- Whether you intend to trade as sole trader or whatever.

More information

Notes for guidance : incorporation of new companies
(Available from Registrar of Companies, Companies House, Crown Way, Maindy, Cardiff CF4 3UZ)
Co-operative Development Agency, Broadmead House, 21 Panton Street, London SW1Y 4DR and Industrial Common Ownership Movement, 7/8 Corn Exchange, Leeds LS1 7BP both provide information about setting up a co-operative
British Franchise Association, 75A Bell Street, Henley-on-Thames, Oxon RG9 2BD supplies information about franchising

INCOME TAX

The first rule of working for yourself is that no matter how small your business is you must keep accurate and full records of all the money coming in and going out as the Inland Revenue will be taking a strong interest in what you're up to. There are lots of cash books on the market to help you or you might decide to get an accounting program for your computer. Ask your accountant for advice on the best way of keeping your accounts. Keep copies of all bills you write and keep receipts or bills to show what you have paid out.

Are you really self-employed?

It is important to check that you really do count as self-employed in your business – it makes a difference as to how much tax you will pay. Simply saying you are self-employed is not enough: you have to satisfy the Inland Revenue that you actually *are*. Basically, if you get a pension, sick pay or holidays from a firm or if you work mainly for one firm in their office and at times and on jobs decided by them, the chances are that the Inland Revenue will decide that you are an employee. On the other hand if you can decide how, when and whether you will do a job, can subcontract work out to others, provide your own equipment and premises, stand to bear any losses you make and are in control of what you do, you are likely to be classed as self-employed.

Working out your tax bill

Whatever form your self-employment takes, you have to pay tax only on your *profit*. Broadly speaking this is your takings less the cost of raw materials, the allowable expenses involved in your work, and various other allowances – capital allowances, personal pension plan premiums, any business losses from previous years, and half the amount you pay in class 4 National Insurance contributions (see below).

Not all the money you spend can be set against your takings. The general rule is that you can claim anything spent 'wholly and exclusively' for the purpose of your work. There are not many hard-and-fast rules about what is and what is not allowed, and you may have to negotiate with the Inland Revenue over some of your expenses. There is a good list of what you are likely to be able to claim in the *Which? Tax Saving Guide* published each March. It is well worth having a look at a copy as it may help you even if an accountant is dealing with your tax affairs.

You are not allowed to claim the whole cost of buying large items of equipment such as machinery or cars in one year. Instead you claim what are called 'capital allowances', so that, for tax purposes, the expenditure is regarded as being split over several tax years.

With items you use partly for business and partly privately (e.g. telephone, heating, or a car), you can claim the proportion of the cost that represents your business use. Keep good records of how the use is shared – for example, log phone calls and record how many miles you do on business in your car – so that you can justify how much you are claiming.

How you might pay tax

This will depend on your circumstances:

■ If you do just occasional freelance work on a self-employed basic *and* work for an employer the Inland Revenue may reduce your PAYE code (see page 30) to collect the tax due on your freelance earnings along with the tax on your earnings from your job. If they tax you each year on the freelance earnings you had the previous year that is fine. But if they guess what your earnings are going to be you could be paying too much (or too little) tax throughout the year and have to pay extra at the end of the year or claim a rebate. If this happens, try to see if you can persuade the Inland Revenue to treat you as self-employed for your freelance earnings (see above).

■ If your self-employed earnings are small and you do not also work for an employer, the Inland Revenue may collect the tax by sending you a bill in December for the current tax year, e.g. in December 1987 you would get a bill for your earnings in the 1987–88 tax year. Because the tax year has not finished, the Inland Revenue will have estimated what your earnings will be. If you do not agree with what they say, you have to write back within 30 days appealing against the estimate by saying why you think it is wrong and asking to postpone paying the tax. This is important.

■ If your self-employed earnings are closely related to your main job – for example if you are a teacher who earns extra by marking exam papers – you are likely to find that the tax due will have already been deducted from your spare-time earnings before you get them under PAYE.

■ If your self-employed earnings are substantial, or are higher than earnings from a job, the Inland Revenue will usually treat you as a fully-fledged business – see below.

A fully fledged business

This is where things become rather complicated. The first

complication is that your accounting year need not run from 6 April of one year to 5 April of the following year to coincide with the tax year. Nor need it coincide with the calendar year. Because of the way you pay your tax it is often best to ensure that your accounting year ends shortly after the end of the tax year – the end of April or May (your very first accounting period can be longer or shorter than 12 months). The reason for this is that from the fourth year you are in business, you will pay tax on a preceding-year basis – your tax bill will be based on the profits made in the accounting year which finished in the preceding tax year. For instance, if your accounting year ends on 30 April, your tax bill for 1987–88 will be based on your profit for the year from 1 May 1985 to 30 April 1986. The tax has to be paid in two instalments – in this example on 1 January 1988 and 1 July 1988.

There are special rules for the first three years. In the first tax year you are in business, you pay tax on the profit you actually make during that tax year. In the second tax year you pay tax on the profit made in the first 12 months your business was running and in the third you can move to the preceding-year basis. (If you prefer, you can have your tax bills for the second and the third year based on the actual profits made in each tax year.) There are special rules for the last three years, too.

More information

IR56 Tax: Employed or self-employed?
IR28 Starting in business
IR57 Thinking of working for yourself?
(All available from your local tax office)

VAT (Value Added Tax)

If your turnover (that is your sales, not your profits) is more than a certain amount in a year you have to be registered for VAT. You will then have to add 15% tax to the cost of most goods and services you provide and hand it over to the Customs and Excise. But you can usually reclaim any VAT you have to pay on goods or services you buy for your business.

In the 1987–88 tax year you have to register for VAT if the turnover of your business (or businesses if you have more than one) is more than £7,250 in any quarter, or more than £21,300 in the past four quarters, or if you have reason to believe that it will be greater than £21,300 in the next 12 months. If any of these apply, get in touch with the VAT office straight away – there are heavy penalties for not registering if you should.

There is nothing to stop you registering for VAT if your turnover is lower than these limits. If you do you will be able to reclaim VAT you pay out for your business and it may be worth doing if you will be dealing mainly with other businesses and pay lots of bills which have VAT added. But the general public can't reclaim the VAT you charge so if your business will be mainly with them, your prices may be higher than other non-registered traders so you could lose trade. And you have the hassle of dealing with the VAT authorities (and suffering penalties if you don't do it properly).

More information

Should I be registered for VAT?
The ins and outs of VAT
The VAT guide
(All available from your local VAT office)

NATIONAL INSURANCE CONTRIBUTIONS

Just as employed people have to pay National Insurance contributions unless they earn a low wage, so do those who are self-employed. You will have to pay the following:

- Class 2 flat rate contributions of £3.85 a week in the 1987–88 tax year. If your earnings are likely to be below a certain amount (£2,125 in the 1987–88 tax year) you can be exempted from paying these. You can pay by buying a stamp from the Post Office each week and stamping it on a contribution card supplied by the DHSS or by direct debit to the DHSS from your bank account.

- Class 4 contributions are based on your profit and are collected by the Inland Revenue along with your tax. In the 1987–88 tax year you will pay 6.3% of your profits between £4,590 and £15,340. Class 4 contributions are simply an extra tax and do not entitle you to anything in the way of benefits.

More information

NI41 *National Insurance guide for the self-employed*
NI27A *People with small earnings from self-employment*
NP18 *Class 4 National Insurance contributions*
(All available from your local DHSS office)

INSURANCE

Just as you need insurance for your home and its contents, for your car and so on, your business needs insurance too.

- If you are working from home, make sure you tell the insurance companies who insure your home and possessions what you are doing. You may have to pay extra premiums.
- If you are using your car for business, tell the insurers. Again, the premium may increase. Also let them know if anyone else will be driving the car in connection with the business, for instance your spouse or employees.
- If you have separate business premises insure them against the same risks as your home – see page 85.
- Insure any business equipment or materials.
- Employer's liability insurance is needed by law if you employ anyone other than members of your own family.
- Public liability insurance may be necessary in case someone is injured by you or by one of your employees in the course of business.
- Product liability or professional negligence insurance can cover any claims for injury or loss due to a faulty product or your negligence in providing clients with poor service or advice.
- You can also consider taking out permanent health insurance (page 123) and/or private patients insurance (page 125).

TAKING ON EMPLOYEES

If your business is, or becomes, large you will no doubt become an employer. There are many duties on employers – keeping up with the paperwork to do with PAYE tax, National Insurance, sick and maternity pay, as well as keeping to the law on employment rights and health and safety. Chapter 4 gives information on many of the rights of employees, and will give you an idea of what you are taking on.

You need to get in touch with the Inland Revenue and DHSS to sort out how you will operate the PAYE system. You should also ensure you have the necessary insurance. Help may be available with the cost of paying wages – for instance under the Young Workers Scheme – and a chat with your local Job Centre should provide the information. They should also be able to provide you with the various Department of Employment leaflets which describe the rights of employees and responsibilities of employers.

More information

P7 Employer's guide to PAYE
(Available from your local tax office)
NP15 Employer's guide to National Insurance contributions
NI227 Employer's guide to statutory sick pay
(Both available from your local DHSS office)

6. Income if you are not earning

In this chapter you will find brief information on the help (mainly financial) available if you are not actually earning at work – whether it is because you are unemployed, ill or disabled, or because you are looking after someone who is ill or disabled. It is laid out in sections according to the reason why you are not working (e.g. because you have lost your job) but there are several general points which cover all the sections:

- As well as the specific state benefits available for different groups of people, there are general 'topping-up' benefits (see page 61) which you may be able to claim if you do not qualify for a specific benefit, or even in addition to such benefits.
- Finding your way through the benefits maze is not easy, especially if you are unhappy with a decision of the DHSS. You can get free professional advice from a number of places including Citizens Advice Bureaux, Disabled Advice Bureaux, and so on.
- The figures for the amounts of money you can get are those for the 1987-88 tax year. The figures usually change each year.
- Some benefits are taxable and you have to give details of what you have received on any tax return you fill in.

IF YOU ARE UNEMPLOYED

If you have just lost your job you should claim unemployment benefit straight away. To get this you must be available for work (this means that you must be prepared to accept any suitable job that is offered and be able to start straight away). Every fortnight you have to sign a declaration that you are available for work –

commonly called 'signing on'. Men over 60 can get benefit without being available for work.

You can be disqualified from getting unemployment benefit for up to 13 weeks if you left your job without a good reason or were sacked for misconduct. If this happens you can appeal against the decision.

Even if you are available for work you will get unemployment benefit only if you have paid enough National Insurance contributions of the right sort at the right time. Only full-rate Class 1 contributions (paid by employees) count.

How much?

You can receive £31.45 a week for up to 52 weeks. You can also claim an increase for one adult dependant who is:

- your husband or wife, as long as he or she doesn't earn more than the increase;
- a separated or divorced husband or wife as long as you are paying him or her maintenance of at least the increase;
- your partner (whether you are living together as husband or wife or living with someone of the same sex) as long as he or she looks after a child of yours for whom you get child benefit, and he or she is not earning more than the increase;
- someone you pay to look after a child for whom you get child benefit (but you must pay him or her at least as much as the increase).

For unemployment benefit the increase is £19.40 a week. (The same rules for claiming for an adult dependant apply to some of the other benefits in this chapter, though the amounts of the increase are different in each case.)

If you are over pension age (60 for women and 65 for men) you can get extra benefit for any dependent children, and the amounts of benefit you get for yourself and for an adult dependant are higher.

Tax

Unemployment benefit is taxable. But if you start claiming during a tax year in which you have earned some money from a job, the chances are that you will not owe any tax. This is because under the PAYE system (see page 30) you may have paid more tax on your earnings than you need have. You will get a rebate either when you get another job (as long as it is within the same tax year) or after the end of the tax year.

Enterprise allowance

Once you have been unemployed for at least eight weeks you can apply for a weekly allowance to help you set up a business – you must be getting either unemployment or supplementary benefit when you apply. You must also have at least £1,000 to invest in the business (you needn't actually have cash – a signed agreement from a relative or your bank agreeing to lend you the money is just as good). Another important condition is that you must not already be running the business. There are a number of rules for getting on the scheme – your local Job Centre will be able to give you full information.

You will be given some training in running a business and a weekly grant of £40 a week for a year. The allowance is taxable.

More information

NI12 Unemployment benefit
(Available from your local DHSS or CAB)
EPL124 Enterprise Allowance Scheme : A guide
EPL140 The Enterprise Allowance Scheme
(Both available from your local Job Centre)
IR41 Income tax and the unemployed
(Available from your local tax office)

IF YOU ARE OFF WORK SICK

There are various benefits for sick people, depending on your circumstances and how long you have been ill. Employed people earning £39 a week or more get statutory sick pay (SSP) from their employer (this is covered on page 35); if you earn less than this, but were earning more in the past, you may be able to claim sickness benefit from the DHSS. You can also claim sickness benefit if you are off work because of an accident or illness related to your work (i.e. it is an industrial injury or illness) and do not earn enough to get SSP, or if you are self-employed.

SSP and sickness benefit last for 28 weeks. If you are still off work at the end of this period, you get invalidity benefit.

State sickness benefit

You will get this only if you have paid enough National Insurance contributions. Full Class 1 contributions paid by employees, and Class 2 paid by self-employed people, count. (If you are suffering from an industrial illness or injury and you do not qualify for SSP you will get sickness benefit even if you have paid no contributions at all.) Sickness benefit is not taxable.

How much

You will get £30.05 for yourself and can claim an increase of £18.60 for one adult dependant (see the list under unemployment benefit on page 55). If you are over pension age you can get extra for your children and the amounts paid are higher. Sickness benefit can be paid for up to 28 weeks.

Invalidity benefit

After you have been getting SSP or sickness benefit for 28 weeks you will move on to invalidity benefit. If you were getting SSP your employer should give you a transfer form which you have to send to the DHSS to claim. If you were getting sickness benefit, you will be transferred automatically to invalidity benefit.

How much?

Invalidity benefit is paid in two parts: invalidity pension and invalidity allowance. Invalidity pension is £39.50 a week. You can also claim an increase for an adult dependant (see unemployment benefit, page 55). You will get the increase for a dependant who lives with you as long as he or she earns no more than £31.45 a week; if the dependant does not live with you, he or she must earn no more than the amount of the increase. Note that the amount a dependant can earn is higher than with sickness benefit, so you might now qualify for it even if you did not when you were getting sickness benefit – so make sure you claim again. You can also claim £8.05 for each dependent child (generally one who lives with you and for whom you or your partner claims child benefit). But if your spouse or partner earns more than a certain amount you will not be able to get any extra for a child.

How much you get in invalidity allowance depends on your age when you first became ill and started claiming SSP or sickness benefit. If you were under 40 you get £8.30, £5.30 if you were between 40 and 49, and £2.65 if you were 50 or more but under 60 (for a man) and 55 (for a woman).

Once you claim invalidity benefit you can go on receiving it until five years beyond normal pension age (until 70 for a man and 65 for a woman).

Tax

Invalidity benefit is not taxable. Because of this, when you reach state pension age (60 for a woman, 65 for a man) you will be better off if you continue to get invalidity benefit than if you opt for your state pension, which is taxable.

More information

FB2 Which benefit?
FB28 Sick or disabled?
FB15 Injured at work
NI16 Sickness benefit
NI16A Invalidity benefit
(All available from your local DHSS or CAB)

IF YOU ARE DISABLED OR PERMANENTLY ILL

There is a lot of help available for people who are suffering from long-term or chronic illness or are disabled. Much of the financial help does not depend on your income: if your condition meets the rules, you get the help.

Severe disablement allowance (SDA)

You may be able to get SDA if you are seriously ill or severely disabled and do not qualify for sickness or invalidity benefit. To qualify you must:

- have been unable to work for 28 weeks or more;
- be very seriously disabled, or get attendance or mobility allowance (see below);
- have lived in Britain for at least ten out of the last twenty years.

If you qualify you will get £23.75 a week and can claim an increase of £14.20 for an adult dependant. The rules for the increase are the same as for invalidity benefit (see above). You can also claim £8.05 for each dependant child but only if your spouse or partner earns less than a certain amount. SDA is not taxable.

Mobility allowance

This is a benefit paid to people who are unable to walk or who have great difficulty in getting about on their own two feet. To get it you will have to show that:

- you are unable to walk, or have great difficulty in walking about out of doors;
- you are likely to remain in the same condition for at least a year.

You can't claim if you are 66 or more (and if you claim when you are 65 you have to persuade the DHSS that you would have qualified before your 65th birthday) or for a child under 5. But if you do get mobility allowance it will be paid until you are 75.

There is room for a lot of argument about whether or not your lack of mobility is enough to qualify you for the allowance. If you do have difficulty walking it is worth claiming. If your claim is refused you can appeal and will then go before a medical board.

If you qualify you will get £22.10 a week which is not taxable.

Attendance allowance

If you, or someone you help look after, need frequent help in order to be able to eat, get dressed, wash and so on or need a lot of looking after to avoid danger, you may be able to claim attendance allowance. You can't claim for a child under 2 and if you are claiming for a child between 2 and 16 the amount of attention or supervision needed must be a lot more than what is normally needed by a child of the same age.

As with mobility allowance there's lots of room for argument over whether the amount of attention needed is frequent, when it's needed or how much supervision is required. Again it is a good idea to seek advice if you have problems claiming the allowance.

Once you qualify you will get £21.20 a week if you need attendance or supervision only at night *or* during the day, and £31.60 if it is needed both night and day. It can be paid for the rest of your life, though the DHSS might make a payment for a shorter length of time so making you re-apply at the end of the period. Attendance allowance is not taxable.

More information

NI252 *Severe disablement allowance*
NI211 *Mobility allowance*
HB4 *Help with mobility*
NI205 *Attendance allowance*
(All available from your local DHSS or CAB)
Disability Rights Handbook
(Your local reference library probably has a copy or write to Disability Alliance, 25 Denmark Street, London WC2H 8NJ)

IF YOU ARE LOOKING AFTER SOMEONE WHO IS ILL OR DISABLED

If you are caring for someone who gets attendance allowance you may be able to get invalid care allowance. To qualify you really need to be looking after him or her every day and for at least 35 hours a week, though in practice you won't have a lot of difficulty proving this. In addition you must not be 'gainfully' employed or in full-time education, though the rules allow you to earn £12 a week. You should also be under pension age, though there are exceptions to this rule.

If your claim is successful you will receive £23.75 and you may be able to get an increase of £14.20 for a dependent adult (see unemployment benefit, page 55) and £8.05 for each dependent child. Invalid care allowance is taxable except for any paid for a dependent child. A married woman can set her married woman's personal allowance against her allowance so is unlikely to owe any tax on her allowance.

More information

NI212 Invalid care allowance
(Available from your local DHSS or CAB)

TOPPING-UP BENEFITS

No matter what other benefits or allowance you get you may also be able to get your income topped-up to ensure that you can at least meet the most basic costs of living:

- Until April 1988 you may be able to claim supplementary benefit.
- From April 1988 you may be able to claim income support.

Supplementary benefit

The rules and regulations are very complicated so only the basic outlines of the scheme are described here. The first rule is that many people have to be available to work and sign on as unemployed (see unemployment benefit, page 54) before being able to claim supplementary benefit. But there are exceptions, the main ones being if you are:

- over 60;
- a single parent with a child under 16;
- expecting a baby within the next 11 weeks;
- ill or disabled.

Supplementary benefit is 'means-tested'; that is, how much you get (indeed whether you get it at all) depends on how much money you have coming in each week. If you are married or living with someone as husband and wife only one of you can claim benefit at the same time, and both your incomes will be added together when working out whether you can get benefit or not (same-sex couples escape this limitation). The DHSS are strict about who they consider to be living together – if they decide you are and you don't agree, get advice. You may be able to persuade them you are two single people.

Your savings

You can't get supplementary benefit if you have more than £3,000 in savings. 'You' includes any savings of your partner, or of your children living with you who are under 16, or under 19 and still at school. The DHSS will also want to know how much you would get if you cashed-in any investment-type life insurance policy (see page 122) though they will ignore the first £1,500. (If you are buying your home with an endowment mortgage – see page 76 – only what would be left if the mortgage had been paid off counts as savings.)

And if you have more than £3,000 don't necessarily think that you can spend it quickly and then claim supplementary benefit. Get advice on how you can spend it without the DHSS deciding that you have 'deliberately abandoned resources', in which case you still won't get benefit.

Your needs

Assuming that you do not have too much in the way of savings, the next step is to calculate your 'requirements', i.e. what the Government thinks you need to live on. These vary according to your circumstances.

Your day-to-day living expenses (food, heating bills, clothes and so on) are meant to be covered by your normal requirements. The level for a couple with three children under 11 would be £80.55 a week or £30.40 for a single person without children.

'Additional requirements' are meant to help certain groups who have greater than normal needs. For example, many people can get extra towards their heating bills, or for a variety of reasons if they are sick or disabled.

What 'housing requirements' count depends on whether you own your home or rent it:

- Home owners can get help with their mortgage interest (not with capital repayments on a repayment mortgage, or with life insurance premiums with their endowment mortgage), an allowance to cover maintenance and insurance, and their water rates (General rates are covered by housing benefit: see below on page 63).
- Renters can only get water rates (their rent and general rates are covered by housing benefit see below).

These three sorts of requirements are added together to get your total needs. Then any income you or your spouse or partner get is totalled. Child benefit, and most other social security benefits except mobility and attendance allowance, are included in your income as are any part-time earnings (though you can ignore £4 of these and up to £16 if you are a single parent). If your requirements are greater than your income you will receive the difference as supplementary benefit.

If you are able to claim supplementary benefit you will also get your full rent and your rates paid by housing benefit.

Income support

From April 1988 this replaces supplementary benefit. In many ways it is similar to supplementary benefit: it is means-tested and you can't claim if you have more than a certain amount of savings. And it is worked out in a similar way: your needs are calculated and any income you have deducted: the remainder is paid as benefit.

But there are differences. The savings limit is higher – £6,000 – but if you have more than £3,000 you will be assumed to be getting an income of £1 a week for each £250 over £3,000. Working out your 'needs' is a lot easier as there are far fewer additional requirements. Instead, certain groups have larger basic needs (a 'premium'), for instance disabled people and families. Housing requirements are also simpler – there is no extra allowance for repairs and insurance or water rates. But in many instances the simplicity is at the expense of giving people less money.

Housing benefit

If you receive supplementary benefit or income support your rent and rates will be paid. Until April 1988 you can get the whole of your rates paid; after that you have to pay part of your rates yourself from your basic benefit – probably 20%.

If you are not able to get supplementary benefit or income support because your income or savings are too high you may still get some help towards your rent and rates. For details of help with rent see page 72, for rates page 92.

More information

National Welfare Benefits Handbook
(Available from bookshops or CPAG, 1-5 Bath Street, London
EC1V 9PY. Price £4.50)
SB1 Cash help – how can I claim supplementary benefit?
SB21 How to claim supplementary benefit if you are unemployed
SB8 Supplementary benefit for pensioners; sick and disabled people;
single parents
SB9 Supplementary benefits for unemployed people
SB16 Lump sum payments
SB19 Weekly payments for special needs
(Available from your local DHSS)

7. Income if you are retired

If you have retired from work, or have reached the age when you can start drawing your State pension, this chapter will help you make sure you are claiming all the benefits you should and help you check that your tax affairs are in order. If you are not already retired this chapter isn't really for you – read Chapter 12 to check that you are making the best plans for your retirement.

YOUR PENSION

Almost everyone will get a pension from the State, and many of those who had worked for an employer will also get an occupational pension. And anyone who has worked for him- or herself will get a pension if he or she has contributed to a pension scheme.

Your pension from the State

The main State pensions are described on page 131 to page 135. In addition there are the following:

■ Over-80 pension of £23.75 a week, paid if you are 80 or more and do not qualify for a basic retirement pension of at least that amount.

■ Supplementary pension which is supplementary benefit (see page 61) under a different name.

■ Though not strictly cash, you can get free prescriptions and possibly help with the cost of dental treatment and glasses.

■ You may also be able to get housing benefit to help pay your rent and rates (see pages 72, 93).

The DHSS should send you a form for claiming your State pension about four months before you can start getting them – if they don't, get in touch with the local DHSS and ask for one. It is important to fill in the form even if you want to defer drawing your pension – if you do this, when you do retire your pension will be higher.

State pensions are paid weekly: you can have a book of orders which you have to cash at a post office (you usually have to stick to one post office – you can't just cash your pension where you like) or you can choose to have your pension paid directly into your bank or building society account every four or thirteen weeks. All the state pensions are taxable (except supplementary pension) but tax is not deducted before you get them.

Although you can claim your state pension even if you are still working, if you are a woman under 65 or a man under 70 and you earn more than £75 a week your basic pension will be reduced. But if you are a woman aged 65 or more, or a man aged 70 or more you can go on earning as much as you like and get your full pension.

Your pension from your work

If you have ever worked, when you retire you should get in touch with all your past employers and check whether you will get a pension from them, and if so, how much. If you are a widow or widower you should check whether you will get a pension from where your husband or wife worked in the past. If you have problems with any of them, an adviser from the Occupational Pensions Advisory Service (OPAS) may be able to help; your local CAB will be able to put you in touch with an adviser.

If you have paid contributions to a personal pension plan you should write to the insurance company, or whoever, and say that you want to start drawing your pension.

With either an occupational pension or a personal pension you may be able to give up part of the pension in exchange for a tax-free lump sum – though there are restrictions on how much you are able to exchange. It is up to you to decide whether you want a lump sum and accept a reduced pension. Although you might just want to spend the cash it is worth thinking about whether you could invest it to provide income a little later. For instance, you could use it to buy an annuity or invest it in a single-premium pension plan to pay out an income in a few years' time.

Any occupational pension you get is likely to be taxed under PAYE, and tax due on other income may be collected at the same time (see below). Basic-rate income tax is deducted from personal pension payments before you get the money. If the total deducted over the tax year comes to more than the tax you should pay you should claim a rebate.

More information

FB2 *Retiring?*
NP32 *Your retirement pension*
NP32A *Your retirement pension if you are widowed or divorced*
NP32B *Retirement benefits for married women*
NI92 *Earning extra pension by cancelling your retirement*
NI184 *Over-80 pension*
(All available from your local DHSS or CAB)

INCOME TAX

There are two aspects of income tax you need to know about. One concerns age allowance – the income you can have before paying tax; the other is to do with how your income tax is collected.

Age allowance

If you (or your wife) are 64 or over before the start of a tax year you can claim a higher personal tax-free allowance – age allowance – than younger people. For people who are 79 or more there is an even higher age allowance. But there is a catch: the extra allowance is designed to help the less well-off, so if your income is more than a certain amount your age allowance is reduced progressively according to your income until it is cut to the level of the ordinary tax-free allowance for a single person or married man. For example, in the 1987–88 tax year, you can claim the full age allowance until your income reaches £9,800. If you are married and neither of you is 79 or more, if your income is £11,120 or more you will not get age allowance but just the ordinary married man's allowance. Between these two limits your age allowance is cut as your income rises – and this has the same effect as having to pay extra tax. In effect, over the part of your income where age allowance is being cut you are (in 1987–88) paying tax at 45%, rather than at the basic rate of 27% (see Table 1, page 24 for full details of this.)

When working out whether your income is high enough to lose you age allowance (either partially or totally) you must include the 'grossed-up' amount of any interest paid after deduction of basic-rate tax. For instance, all interest from bank or building society accounts has had the equivalent of basic-rate tax deducted. To find the gross amount you have to multiply the interest you receive by 100 and divide it by 100 minus the current basic rate of tax. So if you received £1,000 of interest from your building society account in 1987–88 the sum would be:

$$\frac{£1,000 \times 100}{(100 - 27)} = £1,369$$

But you can deduct the gross amount of any outgoings which qualify for tax relief (see page 23, 24), e.g. any mortgage interest.

Avoiding the age allowance trap

Paying higher rates of tax on relatively low incomes doesn't seem like a very good idea. If your income is in the region where you are losing age allowance you may be able to reduce your tax bill by reducing your income for tax purposes:

■ If you have money in building society or bank accounts, you should think about moving some of it into tax-free investments, e.g. National Savings Certificates (see page 165).

■ If you give money to someone regularly, for example a grandchild or a charity, do it under a deed of covenant (see page 27). The gross amount covenanted will reduce your total income.

Tax and your pensions

State pensions are paid without tax being deducted. If you have no other income, you are unlikely to owe any tax as the total state pension you get is likely to be below your tax-free allowance. But if you also get an occupational pension you may well have to pay some tax. Any occupational pension will be taxed under PAYE (see page 30) and the Inland Revenue will try to collect the tax due on all your income at the same time. The result of this will be that it looks as if you are paying a very high rate of tax on your occupational pension.

For example, if you are single and get the full basic retirement pension you will get a total of £2,054 in 1987–88. If in addition you also get an occupational pension of £6,000 your total income is £8,054. But you can claim the full age allowance of £2,960 so do not have to pay tax on this much of your income. However, your £2,054 state pension is being paid in full, with no tax deducted. So you will have to pay tax on all but £906 of your occupational pension – that is how much is left of your tax-free allowance.

More information

IR4 Income tax and pensioners
IR4A Income tax – age allowance
IR34 Income tax – PAYE
(All available from your local tax office)

8. Rent or buy?

The first choice you have when you set up home is between renting – where the main problem is finding a property – and buying – in which borrowing the money you need is the major preoccupation. This chapter looks at both.

RENTING

Though most people would like to own their own homes (in Britain two-thirds of homes are owned by the people living in them), renting can have advantages:

- It is often cheaper than buying, and if you are on a low income help is available to help pay the rent (see page 72).
- You have fewer responsibilities for repairs, maintenance and decorating.
- It can make it easier to move around the country quickly.
- You have fewer financial responsibilities.

Finding a home to rent

If the local council regards you as homeless (i.e. you have absolutely nowhere to stay) and as a priority case (if you have children, or are elderly or disabled or have a violent partner), they must, by law, find housing for you. But if you are not in any of these groups you will have to find yourself somewhere to live. You have the option of renting from:

- a private landlord;
- your local council;
- a housing association.

Private landlords

In many areas there is a great shortage of rented accommodation, and what there is may be expensive and not necessarily in a good state. Look in local newspapers, magazines and shop windows, visit estate agents and ask friends and relatives. If an agency tries to charge you a fee for registering with them, report them to the local authority – the law allows them to do this only if they have found you somewhere to live and you have moved in.

There are two important rights that are applicable to most tenants:

- The right to have a fair rent set by the rent officer (once set it usually can't be increased for two years).
- You can't be made to leave your home without a court order. If your landlord lives in the same building or provides substantial services such as meals or cleaning, it is easy for him or her to get a court order. But if neither of these applies it is usually possible to be evicted only if you break important terms in your tenancy agreement or are seriously behind with the rent.

The laws governing landlords and tenants are notoriously complicated – there is a great variety of types of tenancies each with its' own set of rules. Your local CAB or Housing Advice Centre will be able to help with any problems.

Local councils

In most parts of the country you could have to wait years for a council house or flat. How long you have to wait depends mainly on your needs. If you have a large family, or are currently living in accommodation which is overcrowded or lacks facilities such as a bathroom, or if you have a disabled partner, the chances are that you will be housed quite quickly. On the other hand, if you are young and single you may not even get on the waiting list. But the position varies widely across the country, so talk to the local housing officer at your council offices.

If you get a council house you have no protection against rent increases – the rent usually goes up each year. But you cannot be evicted without a court order. And once you have been living

in a council house for at least three years you have the right to
buy your home at a discount of up to 60%.

Housing associations

These may be charities that provide homes for renting, and have
waiting lists in the same way as local authorities. Some may
provide homes for particular groups of people, e.g. for the
disabled or elderly. Other housing associations run as a sort of
co-operative to help people to buy their own homes – often the
society will have a large mortgage, and all the people who live in
the homes will pay their share of it and will build up a stake in
their own home. Finance is often provided by local authorities
or the Housing Corporation (the body that supervises the
housing associations).

Help with rent

The housing benefit scheme, run by local authorities, is
designed to help tenants pay their rent – whether they are
employed, unemployed, disabled, retired or simply on a low
income. How much you get depends on your income, your
family circumstances and your rent. As examples, if you earn
less than the amounts shown in Table 2 (before any deductions
for tax and so on) you should get some help towards your rent.
(The figures apply to the 1987–88 tax year). Your local Housing
Advice Centre or CAB will be able to work out whether or not
you qualify.

Table 2   Calculating eligibility for housing benefit.

Rent	Single person at work	Couple, one at work, two children	Single parent at work, one child	Retired couple	Couple, one at work, one disabled
	£	£	£	£	£
30	119	172	157	126	148
40	137	190	175	144	166
50	155	208	193	162	184

The figures are weekly amounts.

More information

The rights to buy your council house
(Available from your local council)
One parent families : help with housing
The Rent Act and you : A brief guide
(Both available from your local CAB)

BUYING YOUR OWN HOME

It may not occur to you to ask why you should buy your own home; you may just take it for granted that it is a good thing. In fact, it makes good financial sense for most people. Why?

- Buying your own home is a good investment – over the years house prices have kept well ahead of inflation. But if you want to release part of your investment you may have to buy a smaller home.
- The Government pays part of the cost of buying your home by allowing you tax relief on any mortgage.

Taking on a mortgage

Few people can afford to buy a house outright; almost everyone needs to borrow at least some of the cost. For such an important loan – usually lasting as long as 25 or 35 years, running into tens of thousands of pounds and taking up a large slice of your income in repayments – lenders want to make sure that their money is particularly safe. So a loan to buy a house is almost always in the form of a mortgage: in return for lending you the money, the lender has the right to repossess your home and sell it if you do not keep up the repayments. In the jargon, the home is 'security' for the loan; to put it another way, the loan is 'secured' on your home.

There are two questions a lender will ask when deciding whether or not to give you a mortgage:

- Can you afford to make the repayments on the loan?
- Is the property worth enough to cover the loan if you don't keep up the repayments?

Can you afford the repayments?

It is up to the lender to decide what you can afford to repay –
normally based on how much you earn. A single person can
usually reckon on a loan of between two-and-a-half to three
times his or her yearly salary – so a weekly wage of £150 would
allow you to borrow up to £23,400; a salary of £15,000 a year up
to £45,000.

A couple where both are earning tend to get a bit less than
they would as two separate people. You can usually borrow
about two-and-a-half to three times the higher of the two
incomes plus one to one-and-a-half times the lower income.
Alternatively, you might get two to two-and-a-half times the
sum of your two incomes.

These days it is illegal to discriminate against women. And
lenders are much less concerned about what sort of a couple you
are – married or unmarried, same sex or different sexes – but
you may need to shop around more carefully to get the best
terms for your situation. But a group of people buying together
may find mortgages a little more difficult to get, and won't get
anything like as big a loan as their joint incomes would
suggest.

But simply because you can find a lender who is prepared to
lend you, say, three-and-a-half times your income, do not
assume you can really afford this. Check your own situation
carefully. Do you have particularly high travelling costs, for
instance? Might your income drop soon – if you have to look
after a relative, or children ? Or are you gambling too much on
your earnings rising far and fast?

Is the property worth enough?

If you can't keep up the repayments on your mortgage, the
lender will recover the money by taking back your home and
selling it.

Selling a home costs money, and a repossessed home often
fetches less than similar properties: they are often in poor
condition (if you have not been able to keep up the mortgage,
you are unlikely to have been able to keep up the maintenance
either): and the lender will want to sell quickly – maybe even for
a lower price than the real value of the house. So the lender is
unlikely to lend you the full purchase price of the home you
want to buy – even if this is well within the amount you can

afford to repay. Instead, you'll be restricted to a percentage often no more than 75% or 80%. You will have to provide the rest from your own savings or from whatever you've got left over after selling a previous home.

This is hard on first-time buyers, and on those moving from areas where housing is cheap to where it is more expensive. So many lenders will let you have a higher percentage than normal (sometimes up to 100%, especially if you are a first-time buyer and not after a very expensive property) if you can let them have extra security over and above the property itself.

You could offer anything as security that could be turned into sufficient cash if the need arose. That usually means property again – but few people who actually need 100% loans have the odd holiday cottage as well. But fortunately, a special sort of insurance – a 'mortgage indemnity policy' is suitable security. This guarantees to compensate the lender if the sale of your home did not cover the amount of the loan. You pay a single fee (premium) at the time you take out the mortgage – perhaps 3% of the amount of the loan over the lender's normal limit.

There is a further problem. The amount you can borrow is a percentage of what the lender's valuer reckons the home is worth; that could be less than the purchase price, so even a 100% mortgage might not be enough if you have no savings.

Types of mortgage

There are two main elements in paying off any sort of loan: you have to pay back the amount you borrowed (the 'capital') and you have to pay the cost of actually borrowing the money (the 'interest'). There are two basic types of mortgage loan:

- With a repayment mortgage, you pay the going rate of interest *plus* a little bit of the capital each month until eventually there is no more capital to repay and the loan comes to its end.
- With an endowment mortgage you pay only the interest, but you also take out a life insurance policy involving a regular saving scheme which is intended to be worth enough eventually to repay the capital in one lump sum. There are other types of mortgage which work in a similar way.

Repayment mortgage

Although you pay both interest and capital, in the first few years most of your payment goes to cover the interest, and the amount of capital you repay is very small. But over the years, as the capital you owe decreases the amount of interest decreases too, and in turn this allows more of each payment to go towards capital repayment until in the last couple of years of the mortgage, very little of your payment is interest.

In general, lenders try to keep the amount of your monthly repayments the same throughout the length of the mortgage. (That is, assuming interest rates stay the same). This means you know in advance what your monthly outgoings will be and when you will have paid off the loan. A mortgage designed for constant repayments in this way, after taking into account tax relief (see page 81), is called a 'level repayment' type.

With an increasing repayment mortgage your repayments, before taking into account tax relief, are constant. The advantage is that you get more tax relief in the early years of the loan (because interest makes up almost all your repayments to start with). So the amount you actually have to pay out each month is lower in the early years. In later years the amount of tax relief falls so your repayments increase and overtake those of a level repayment mortgage but by then your mortgage repayments will be a much smaller part of your income so that a slight increase will hardly be noticed.

Even if you have no other insurance on your life, you should take out some to cover the mortgage if you have dependants or if you are buying the house as a couple. A mortgage protection policy is a relatively cheap form of life insurance, because you get only enough to pay back the outstanding amount of the loan if you die (and nothing back if you live long enough to pay off the mortgage). But it relieves your dependants and partner from the major worry of making sure they keep a roof over their heads.

Endowment mortgage

The interest part of an endowment mortgage is simple – you just pay the lender the going rate of interest, less any tax relief. But there are many variations on the endowment policy (the savings part) theme.

The simplest type is the non-profit policy which guarantees to pay out enough to cover the capital you borrowed – but that is all.

A with-profits endowment policy guarantees to pay at least enough to pay off the mortgage, but there is a possibility that there will be quite a lot left after the mortgage is paid. The costs are higher than for a non-profit policy, and in effect it is just enforced savings (which may or may not be a good investment) for the life of the mortgage. Do not be taken in by the huge projected profits – remember that inflation will cut them down to size. Also bear in mind that the company won't guarantee that you will make all this extra money.

A low-cost policy is also a with-profits policy. But at the outset you are guaranteed to make enough to pay off only about half the mortgage: the potential profits are estimated to be enough to at least cover the other half. This may sound a bit risky but it is not really. The lender will want to make sure the company is sound, and the money pretty well safe; and may also want a further insurance guarantee to help spread the risk of failure. A low-cost endowment policy costs quite a bit less each month than a with-profits or non-profits policy.

You do not need separate life insurance – all endowment policies include insurance to pay off the capital if you die before the end of the mortgage.

Other types of mortgage

Two other types of mortgage work in a similar way to endowment mortgages. With a pension mortgage, instead of taking out an insurance policy to provide the funds for paying off the capital, you make payments into a pension plan. When you retire, you use part of the lump sum that the pension plan provides to pay off the mortgage. Pension mortgages have the advantage that you get tax relief on the contributions to the pension plan, as well as on the mortgage interest payments. So they are very tax-efficient, particularly if you are a higher-rate taxpayer. But your pension will be reduced because part of your fund has been used to pay off the mortgage. Life insurance is not included: if you want it, you have to buy it separately. From 1988 a pension mortgage is available to everyone who opts for a personal pension scheme rather than the state or an employer's pension (see Chapter 13). Before then only those who are self-employed or not a member of an employer's pension scheme are eligible.

With a unit-linked mortgage, a unit-trust-type investment, in shares say, is used to provide the capital to pay off the mortgage. This is definitely a much riskier business; not all lenders will consider it, and some may require a guarantee that the investment will pay out enough to cover the loan.

Which to choose?

A basic repayment mortgage has the advantage that it is straightforward and has the lowest monthly payments (when interest rates are around 10% or higher) If you move house, there is no problem in paying off one mortgage and taking out another. If you can't afford the repayments, there is some scope for manoeuvre (see page 82). An increasing repayment mortgage, if you can get one, is likely to be best for most people: you get all the advantages outlined above, plus lower monthly payments in the early years, when cost matters most.

The main problem with any other type of mortgage is that you are linking your mortgage to a long-term investment that might prove inflexible if your circumstances change. If you move, the existing investment might not be enough to cover the new mortgage, and you would have to take out another one. If you decide to change your type of mortgage, you may not want to continue with the investment – but cashing it in, especially if it's fairly new, is not likely to be financially worth while. If you can't afford the mortgage there's much less scope for negotiations than with a repayment mortgage (see page 83).

Only at low rates of interest is a repayment mortgage likely to be more expensive than any other type and then it is beaten only by a low-cost endowment mortgage, on which there is no guarantee that you will get enough to pay off the capital. If you are arranging a personal pension plan *and* you are sure you can afford to lose part of your pension to pay off the mortgage when you retire it is worth considering a pension mortgage.

More mortgage for your money

If you need to borrow more than the normal rules allow for your income, there are several possibilities which may help:

- **Index-linked loan**. The interest rate and your repayments start off low but then rise from year to year along with the rise in an index – perhaps of prices in general or of house prices. If your income keeps up with the index, your repayments as a proportion of your income will remain the same. But if your income were to fall behind the index you could find yourself in real trouble, paying out a greater and greater proportion of your income in repayments, and possibly ending up owing more than your house is worth.

- **Shared ownership schemes** (run by some housing associations and local authorities). You own only part of your home; on the rest you pay rent. This can help first-time buyers to get on the housing ladder, and as time goes by and your income increases you can buy more of the share in your house.

- **Low-start schemes**. These allow you to make smaller payments in the early years of a mortgage – and of course then require larger payments in later years, to make up.

- **Long-life mortgages**. These last more than the usual 15 to 25 years. The monthly payments are lower – but you end up paying interest for a longer period, and so your total payments are larger; 30-year mortgages are quite common, 35-year ones less so. You may find 'whole life' mortgages designed not to be paid off until you finish work: for a 20-year-old this could mean a mortgage of 45 years. If you are worried about the total amount of interest you have to repay on a long-life mortgage, remember that with a repayment mortgage you can always increase your monthly payments when you can afford to, and so reduce the length of the loan.

- **Discounts** (a cut in the interest rate, usually for first-time borrowers). These are rarely large enough or last long enough to make a difference to the amount you can borrow but they can help when you are first setting-up home, and you are sure you can't get your mortgage cheaper elsewhere anyway.

- **Government Homeloan scheme**. If you are hoping to buy your first home in a couple of years' time, look at this scheme: if you save regularly and buy a cheap enough home you can get a cash grant of £110, and an interest-free loan of up to £600.

- **Guaranteed mortgages**. In return for saving regularly you are guaranteed a loan linked to the amount you've saved; you might not get much in the way of interest, but the loan is a help if money for mortgages is in short supply.

Interest rates

The interest you pay on most mortgages varies as interest rates in the economy change. Some lenders ask borrowers to change their repayments every time rates change; others alter them once a year to take account of changes in the previous year. This is good when interest rates rise as your payments will stay the same until the following year. But if they fall, you will not have more money to spend – in effect you will be paying off your mortgage more quickly.

Most lenders quote interest rates in a standard way by giving you the APR (annual percentage rate). This includes not only the interest you pay but the things you have to pay for when setting up the mortgage such as valuation fees. But it doesn't include the cost of any compulsory insurance policies, so you should also look at monthly repayments if you want to compare different lenders' terms.

Where to buy

Shop around: you do not just have to go to the bank or the building society where you have been a saver. Look at the following:

- **Building societies**. Though building societies are developing new products, lending money to buy homes will remain very much their main business, and there is little chance that they won't be around in future years if you want a new or bigger loan. If you save or have a mortgage with a society, you're more likely to get money at a time when mortgages are restricted (though the theme these days is to ensure there's enough money for everyone – mortgage queues are supposed to be a thing of the past).
- **Banks** (both the big high-street names, and less well known UK branches of foreign banks). These are the other major mortgage providers. There is little to choose between their terms and those of a building society although banks tend to have higher minimum loans than building societies and may have higher upper limits.

- **Other lenders.** These are either much less important in the market, or have drawbacks. Some employers offer mortgages, perhaps as a fringe benefit of the job. This is a good buy if the interest rate is lower than normal. But find out first what will happen if you leave the firm: will they let you keep on the loan, and on what terms?

  Insurance companies are unlikely to offer anything but standing mortgages, probably linked to their own endowment policy or pension scheme. Don't expect them to be wholly unbiased in their advice as to the type of mortgage you should go for, or the best investment to link a standing mortgage to.

  Finance houses and credit companies are keen to lend money – most charge higher rates than normal. Again, they are less likely to offer repayment mortgages. Watch the terms and conditions carefully: might you have to pay heavy penalties if you pay off the mortgage in its early years?

  Local authorities lend almost exclusively to people wanting to buy their own council houses. But some authorities have run schemes to lend, say, to people doing up derelict houses. And occasionally they have a bit of money to spare for other borrowers.

  Mortgage brokers or insurance brokers are most likely to want to fix you up with a standing mortgage, because they'll get commission from the investment company they recommend. Similarly, they may be less likely to recommend insurance companies who don't pay commission (Ecclesiastical Insurance Equitable Life, London Life) than those who do. If they arrange a repayment mortgage, you may have to pay them a fee. There is not much point in using a broker if you want a simple mortgage and have the stamina to shop around yourself. Even if you do use a broker, it is worth checking their recommendations – perhaps by seeing what another broker would offer.

Tax relief

As a way of borrowing, a mortgage is very cheap. This is partly because the lenders have to take very little risk – they have your house as security for their loan. But a big reason for the cheap cost to you is that mortgages to buy or improve your main home are subsidised by the Government in the form of tax relief on the interest payments you make. This means that the interest you pay is reduced by the level of basic-rate tax (whether you pay tax or not). For example, if the basic tax rate is 27p in the £, for every £100 of interest the lender wants, you pay only £73 and the Government makes up the other £27. (In terms of interest rates, it means that a quoted rate of 10% really only costs you 7.3%).

This scheme is called MIRAS, standing for 'Mortgage *I*nterest *R*elief *A*t *S*ource'. Most borrowers will get their tax relief in this way although some who borrowed more than £30,000 before April 1987 may not, as lenders did not have to operate MIRAS for these loans then. If you are not in MIRAS, ask the lenders whether they will allow you to be.

If you pay tax at higher rates you claim extra tax relief: each year when you complete your tax return you need to send in a certificate from your lender showing how much interest you have paid. You will get the extra tax relief either through your PAYE code or by getting a lower tax bill.

You get tax relief only on the interest charged on the first £30,000 of loans – if you borrow more you have to pay the full amount of the interest on the extra. For married couples the limit is £30,000 between them; for joint borrowers who are not married it is £30,000 each.

To get tax relief the loan must be for buying or improving your only (or main) residence, or a home for a former or separated husband or wife, or for a dependent relative. But the limit for all these loans in total is still £30,000.

Problems paying your mortgage?

The first rule is that you should get in touch with the lenders as soon as you start to have problems. Remember they have the right to take court action to repossess your home if you get into arrears. The second thing is to see whether there is any way of increasing your income – there may be benefits you could claim or you may be paying too much tax. Your local CAB or Money Advice Centre would be able to check all these things.

With a repayment mortgage the lender may agree to increase the length of the mortgage – this will decrease the repayments as you have a longer period over which to repay the loan. But in the early years it will not have a big impact on your repayments because most of what you are repaying is interest, not capital. So you may have to see whether the lender is prepared to allow you to pay only the interest part of the mortgage until your finances improve.

With an endowment or other standing mortgage you have less flexibility as you are already paying interest only, and extending the length of the loan will make no difference. In addition you have to keep up the endowment premiums.

With either type, if you are able to claim supplementary benefit or income support (see page 61), your mortgage interest payments will be taken into account when calculating how much benefit you get. But the capital repayments (with an endowment mortgage) or policy premiums (with an endowment mortgage) will not be paid.

Insuring against illness or unemployment

Some mortgage lenders now offer insurance policies which will pay your mortgage if you are not earning because of sickness or unemployment. The cost of the insurance adds around £10 to £12 to the monthly repayments on a £30,000 loan. *Which?* magazine compares costs and cover provided by different insurance companies from time to time; your local library should have a copy.

Before agreeing to take out such a policy you should first read the small print very carefully:

- Check when the policy will pay out. Is it just if you are ill or have an accident and are unable to work, or does it include redundancy? What if you opt for voluntary redundancy or are sacked? The wider the circumstances in which you can claim, the better.

- Check that you work enough hours to be able to claim – some policies will not pay out if you normally work part-time, even if you earn good money in that time. Also watch out if you are self-employed; some policies will pay out only for illness.

- Check that you have been with your employer long enough – some policies will not pay out for redundancy or unemployment if you have been with your employer for less than six months.

- Check for how long your mortgage payments will be met. Most policies pay for only one year and you are unlikely to find a policy which pays for more than two years.

More information

Hints for home buyers
Taxation and the building society borrower
Building societies and house purchase
Building societies and house purchase in Scotland
(All available from the Building Societies Association, 3 Savile Row, London W1X 1AF)
Buying a flat
(from RICS, 12 Great George Street, London SW1P 3AD)
IR63 Mortgage interest relief at source
(Available from your local tax office)
Home sweet home – a guide for first-time buyers
(From Office of Fair Trading (see p. 20) or local Trading Standards Office)

9. Running your home

In this chapter we look at some of the running costs of a home, particularly one that you are buying or own.

INSURING YOUR HOME

Your home is almost certainly the most valuable thing you own and you would be foolish not to insure it against damage, with a house buildings insurance policy. The chances of it being totally destroyed are small but even relatively minor damage can be expensive to repair. *Which?* magazine compares costs and cover from time to time; your local library may have a copy.

If you have a mortgage, the lenders will insist on your having insurance. (They are not thinking of you but are protecting their own stake in your home.) You may not have any choice over the insurance – although building societies are supposed to give you a choice of at least three companies. But even if you have no choice, check the policy carefully and if you feel you need more cover than it gives or you find a cheaper policy you could ask whether the lender would be prepared to let you change insurers. (Beware of being asked to pay an annual charge for this as it could mean it is not worth changing.)

If you are a tenant, you do not usually pay for buildings insurance – your landlord does.

What is covered?

The main job of buildings insurance is to pay out to put right damage done to the structure of your home or to things in it which are permanent fixtures: your bath and other plumbed-in fittings, central heating, fitted kitchen units and so on. It may also cover some damage done outside, for instance to your garage or greenhouse, paths or fences.

All policies cover damage caused by the following:

- Fire, explosions, lightning or earthquakes ('fire' doesn't usually include damage caused simply by smoke).
- Storms and floods.
- Subsidence (when the land your house is on caves in), heave (when it rises) and landslip. Watch out for lots of exclusions – for instance damage caused by normal settlement of land or while you are having building work done.
- Vandals or thieves.

Some policies will cover other types of damage; but all exclude damage caused in certain ways, for example, as a result of poor maintenance, and will probably put limitations on when they will pay out even for the types of damage they cover.

There are one or two other circumstances in which you can make a claim under a buildings policy:

- If your home is so badly damaged that you can't live in it until it has been repaired, you can claim the cost of renting somewhere to live.
- If you are sued for damage which is your responsibility as the owner of your home – for instance for injuries to a tenant caused by your failing to carry out necessary repairs. This is known as 'owner's liability' insurance.
- If you are sued for damage or injury caused by faulty building work that was carried out at a house you used to own.
- If you accidentally damage baths, etc. or glass in windows or doors.

Some policies will pay out for other damage too and you may feel it worth looking out for some or all of these bits of extra cover. For instance some policies cover damage to your heating or water system (including your plumbed-in washing machine or dishwasher) caused by freezing water.

How much does it cost?

This depends on three things:

- The type of insurance cover.
- The rebuilding cost of your home, and so the amount you need to insure for.

- The cost, or premium, the company charges for each unit of cover.

The type of insurance

The cheapest insurance policies are those which give 'indemnity' cover. This means that if you make a claim you will get the cost of the repairs less a deduction for wear and tear. For instance, if your roof had already been on your home for 20 years and was expected to last 60 years you would get only two-thirds of the cost of repairing it. You would do better to pay slightly more and go for a policy that gives 'new-for-old' cover – the best type for most people. If you make a claim you will get the full cost of the repair (assuming you are insured for the correct amount).

Policies that include full 'accidental damage' or 'all risks' cover pay to repair damage caused by accidents such as you putting your foot through the ceiling while working in the loft, or spilling paint over the brickwork while painting the windows outside. However, they are very expensive.

Rebuilding cost

This is the total cost of rebuilding your home and outbuildings, paths, etc. from scratch. It has little to do with what your home is worth in terms of what you could get for it if you sold it – so ignore that figure completely.

It is important to make sure that you are insuring for the correct amount. If it is too low and you make a claim the insurance company may pay less than is needed to do the repairs; too high and you will be paying for more insurance than you need. There are several ways of making sure you insure for the right amount:

- You can work out the rebuilding cost yourself by getting hold of a leaflet published by the Association of British Insurers (see page 88 for the address). But do this only if your home is relatively modern and built of conventional materials.
- You can rely on the figure suggested by your lender's valuer when you bought your home (if you insure through the lender). If you increase this as suggested and tell the lender about any improvements, you should be treated as being fully insured even if the figure does turn out to be too small.

■ You can get a qualified surveyor to tell you how much it would cost to rebuild your home. This may be the only sure way if your house is old or unusual, but you will have to pay for it.

■ You can choose a 'no sum-insured' policy where the premium is not based directly on the rebuilding cost of your home but simply on its size and its type (detached, semi-detached, etc.) and where it is. You are then insured with no limit and there is no danger of being under-insured.

Most policies automatically increase the amount insured (and so the cost) each year in line with increasing rebuilding costs. Beware of policies that do not do this; they could leave you under-insured.

The premium

The rate charged for each £1,000 of rebuilding cost can be anything from around £1.50 to £2.00 for new-for-old cover, and up to £2.50 or more for accidental damage or all-risks cover. With most insurers the cost is the same no matter where you live but some do charge different rates depending on whether you live in a rural or city area. There are other factors which could mean your having to pay more than normal rates:

■ If your home is particularly at risk, e.g. it has a thatched roof or is in an area prone to flooding.

■ If your home is old.

■ If you leave your home unoccupied for long periods.

More information

Buildings insurance for home owners
Claiming on your home insurance policy
(Both available from Association of British Insurers, Aldemary House, Queen Street, London EC4N 1TT)

INSURING YOUR POSSESSIONS

We all value the things we own, not least because it would cost a lot of money to replace them. A house contents policy insurance can take a lot of the worry away, though of course it can't replace family heirlooms or memories brought back by photographs. You should have this insurance whether you are a tenant or own your own home.

What is covered?

A house contents policy usually covers damage to things which are kept in your home, garage or outbuildings. Fixed things that you would expect to leave behind when you move home such as curtain rails and built-in kitchen appliances are not covered as they are included in the buildings insurance.

The basic circumstances in which a policy will pay out are the same as that for buildings insurance – see page 86. You can also claim for the following:

- The cost of alternative accommodation if your home is uninhabitable as a result of damage covered by your policy. If you own your own home, you will be able to claim a higher amount for this under your buildings policy. If you are a tenant look for a contents policy allowing you to claim up to 20% of the total insured for alternative accommodation.
- Some damage to fixtures and fittings if you are a tenant and are responsible for any damage you do to them.
- Some accidental damage – usually limited only to damage to TVs (though not portables), mirrors and glass in furniture.
- Injury or damage for which you are responsible.

Personal liability insurance covers accidents caused by you, your family or your pets. Occupier's liability insurance covers injury or damage caused by your property (for instance a slate falling off your roof and injuring a passer-by). Employer's liability would pay damages to domestic employees who were injured while working at your home.

Some policies offer extra cover which you may want to look for. For instance, it may be useful to have a policy which pays for replacing or repairing accidental damage to your video or home computer. Some policies pay to replace frozen food damaged as a result of a power cut or freezer failure; others give you some cover for your belongings when you move home.

How much does it cost?

This depends on:

- the type of insurance cover you want;
- the value of your belongings;
- where you live.

Types of insurance cover

An 'indemnity' policy pays out the cost of replacing or repairing whatever is damaged or destroyed less a deduction for wear and tear. So if your television has an expected life of ten years, and it is destroyed by fire after five, you would get half the cost of replacing it with a new set and have to pay the rest of the cost yourself. But things which increase in value with age such as antiques are covered for the full replacement cost, as are brand-new things.

A 'new-for-old' policy pays the full replacement or repair cost no matter how old the item. Some policies contain an element of both these types of insurance – giving all or some of your belongings new-for-old cover until they are a certain age, say five years, then switching to indemnity cover.

An 'accidental damage' policy covers the cost of replacing or repairing things damaged accidentally in your home, for instance if you spill paint-stripper on your polished table, and an 'all-risks' policy covers all damage and loss (except for things specifically excluded), in and out of the home. These sorts of cover on all your belongings are unnecessarily expensive for most people.

For most people, a new-for-old policy is the best choice. You can have this extended so that things you take out of the home frequently or might easily lose (such as jewellery, cameras, sports or musical equipment) are covered for accidental damage, or all risks.

Valuing your belongings

If you insure your belongings for much less than they are worth, the insurance company may not pay out the full amount of any claim. There is no advantage in over-insuring as the insurance company will never pay out more than the total value of your belongings so you would be throwing your money away.

You have to insure your belongings for the amount it would cost to replace them all if they were totally destroyed. Guessing isn't much good as you are likely to under-estimate the cost. The only way is to go from room to room listing everything you own and then find out the current shop prices of equivalent items. Do not rely on any guidelines on how much, on average, people have in their houses as your possessions could be far from average. You will need a professional valuation on expensive items, for example for any jewellery or items other than furniture which are worth more than £300 or so.

With a new-for-old policy you must then insure for the cost of replacing everthing. But with an indemnity policy, or a mixed policy, the total will be less as you can deduct wear and tear from the replacement value of individual items.

Where you live

In general, the higher the risk of burglary, the higher the premiums. So inner cities have the highest premiums, rural areas the lowest; Table 3 gives examples:

Table 3   Premiums on house insurance as related to location of house.

Type of policy	Cost per £1,000 of cover	
	Rural village	London suburb
	£	£
Indemnity	2.75	5.50
Mixed	3.00	7.50
New-for-old	3.50	8.50
Accidental damage	5.00	10.00
All-risks	6.00	12.00

Other factors might put up your premium:

- If your home is always unoccupied during the day.
- If you have lots of valuable items.
- If your home is particularly at risk, for instance it has a thatched roof or is in an area prone to flooding.
- If you or anyone else in the house is considered to have a 'risky' job, e.g. as a journalist or an entertainer.
- If you have made lots of claims in the past.

More information

Home contents insurance
Claiming on your home insurance policy
(Both available from the Association of British Insurers, address on page 88)

RATES

Rates are simply a tax which you have to pay for the benefit of occupying your home. The money collected makes up about one-third of the total needed by local authorities for providing services, e.g. education, council housing, police and fire services and rubbish collection.

Your rates bill

Your annual bill is simply your home's rateable value multiplied by the local rate-in-the-pound (see below). For example, if your home is valued at £400 and the local rates are £2 in the £, your rates bill will be £800.

Your rates demand comes in March and you can pay either in one lump sum, in two lump sums in April and October, or in instalments through the year (usually from May to February). In general it is always best to try to spread bills over the whole year, but if you are offered a discount for paying one lump sum at the start of the year, and you have the cash to do so, this could be cheaper. A simple rule of thumb is to pay in one lump if the discount is half or more of the interest rate you could get if you invested the lump sum and used it to pay the rates in instalments.

Rateable value

This is loosely related to how much you would have to pay if you rented your home – or rather, how much you would have paid if you had been renting it at the time of the last revaluation (1973 for England and Wales, 1985 in Scotland). Rateable values vary widely across the country, but the larger your home and the more facilities it has the higher will be its rateable value compared with other houses in the area. If you make improvements to your home or extend it your rateable value may be increased.

If you think your rateable value is too high you can try to get it reduced and so lower your rates bill. In England and Wales you have to show that the valuation is high when compared with similar homes or that a change in the area means that your home is now worth less to someone renting it than it was at the last revaluation. (In Scotland you can only try to get your rateable value reduced just after the revaluation or if there has been a change in the area.)

You fill in a form from your local valuation office (or assessor's office in Scotland), giving details of why you think the value on your house is too high. If the valuation officer doesn't agree, the local valuation court will hear both sides of the case and make a decision on your application. If you get a reduction it is unlikely to be large, but applying does not cost anything (other than your time).

Rates-in-the-pound

Once your local council has drawn up their budget they calculate how much of this has to be financed by the local rates. Then, as they know the total valuation of properties in the area, they can work out the rate-in-the-pound.

Changes on the way

For many years the government has been trying to find a way of replacing the current rating system. Starting in 1989 it is proposed that Scotland will move to a system whereby everyone over 18 will pay a flat-rate 'community charge' that is not related to the housing he or she lives in. The system may be extended to England and Wales later. It would mean that a family with several grown-up children could find their total bill going up, while single people could pay less. To collect the same amount as they currently collect under the rating system, most local authorities would charge between £120 and £250 per person, although in some London boroughs the charge could be £400 per person. The housing benefit scheme (see below) would still help people on low incomes to pay their community charge as it does now with rates.

Can't afford your rates?

If you are on a low income, whether you are working, unemployed, retired or unable to work, you can apply for housing benefit from your local council. How much you get depends on your family circumstances, how much money you have coming in, and your rates bill. If you are getting supplementary benefit or income support (see page 61) you will automatically get financial help to pay your rates. Ask a local advice agency such as a CAB or housing advice centre to check whether you might be eligible.

Whatever your other debts, it is a dangerous practice to fall behind with your rates; local councils can fairly easily get court orders to take away your possessions if you do. Get advice from your local CAB or housing advice centre if you are having problems.

WATER CHARGES

We all pay for the water we use (and for its disposal through the sewage system). Most of the costs involved in supplying water, maintaining the sewers, and flood and pollution control are financed by the charges paid by domestic and commercial users.

Ways of paying

Water charges for domestic users are usually based on the home's rateable value (see above). And like rates you may be allowed to pay the water supplier in instalments throughout the year, rather than in a lump sum at the beginning of the year.

Some water suppliers offer customers the choice of paying for their water by meter so that the bills are more directly related to how much water they use. Whether or not it is worth switching to this method of costing depends on how much water you use, what you pay now and how much it will cost to install the necessary metering equipment. If your suppliers offer the option they will be able to give you some guidance.

Can't afford your water charges?

If you are on supplementary benefit your water rates are taken into account when calculating your benefit. If you do not qualify for supplementary benefit, you won't get any help however low your income is, or however difficult you find it to pay your water charges. And you will not get help under the new income support scheme (see page 63).

Water suppliers can cut your water off if you don't pay the

bills. So if you are having difficulty it is very important to get help and advice. Go along to a CAB or other advice centre to see if there are ways in which your income can be increased – perhaps by claiming benefits you didn't know you could get.

IMPROVING YOUR HOME

A popular pastime for home owners is home improvement: fitting double glazing or a new bathroom or kitchen; adding a conservatory or extension; even landscaping the garden. Don't be misled into thinking that you will necessarily recoup the cost of making these improvements when you sell your home. You may with some: for example by adding central heating or putting in a bathroom where none existed before. But double glazing or an extension may add less than half their cost to the value of the house. Small alterations which improve the appearance of your home can make it easier to sell, for example putting in a modern, well-designed bathroom or kitchen. But in general you should make improvements because you really want the extra facilities or space, rather than because you want to make a profit.

If you are planning major work, such as building an extension or altering the outside of your home, you should contact the planning officers at your local council. They will be able to tell you whether you need planning permission. Even if this is not needed, almost all the work has to conform to building regulations: check before you start with the building control department (again at your local council).

Paying for the work

If you have an older home which needs lots of work to bring it up to modern standards you may be able to get a grant from the local council to help with the cost. Grants are also available to help convert a home into flats. There are three types of grant:

- **Intermediate grants**. These are for putting basic amenities (inside toilet, sink, hot and cold water, etc.) into homes built before 1961. If your home qualifies, the council must give you a grant.
- **Improvement grants**. These are to help with the cost of improving your home to modern standards or for converting

it to flats. The home has to have been built before 1961 and be below a certain rateable value (£400 in Greater London, £225 elsewhere). These grants are discretionary – it is up to your council to decide whether or not you get the money.

- **Repairs grants**. These are to help with the cost of major repairs (re-roofing, for example) to homes built before 1919. Again, the grants are discretionary.

Borrowing

Even if you get a grant, this will not cover the whole cost of improvements. If you need to borrow money you should first ask the company with whom you have your mortgage (if any) and see whether it would be prepared to increase your mortgage with a further advance. The advantages of this are that the loan will be repaid over a long period and the interest rate is likely to be lower than on other loans. Check how much the further advance will cost (there could be surveyor's and legal fees): it could make this way of borrowing expensive if you want only a small amount.

If you do not have a mortgage you could ask banks or building societies whether they would lend you the money. Many have special plans for home improvements. Or if you already have an endowment life insurance policy you may be able to get a loan from the insurance company – you would then pay interest only and repay the loan when the policy pays out.

You can get tax relief (see page 81) on loans for improving your own home provided the total of all your loans for improving and buying your home do not add up to more than £30,000. You can't get tax relief on money you borrow on a credit card or overdraft even if it is for home improvements. And not all improvements count: there is a list in booklet *IR11* which you can get from your tax office (see below).

More information

Planning permission: a guide for householders
Home-improvement grants
(Both available from your local council)
IR11 Tax treatment of interest paid
(Available from your local tax office)

10. In and out of marriage

Most people form relationships or partnerships with another person at some stage in their lives; and many later break them. The most formal relationship is that of marriage, surrounded by many civil and financial laws; similarly, it is the relationship that is most covered by law when it ends – either through divorce or death. So this chapter concentrates on married couples, though there is information for non-married partners too.

GETTING MARRIED

If you are already married or have decided to take the plunge there are ways in which you can plan your finances to save you money. If you are wondering whether or not to tie the knot, this section may help you to make up your mind.

Your tax

When you are married you don't each deal with your own tax affairs. Instead the husband is responsible for the tax affairs of both himself and his wife. Only he will get a tax return and he is legally bound to pay the whole of the tax bill (though in practice a wife who works will pay her own tax under the PAYE system).

Tax-free allowance

Each of you is given a tax allowance so that you can have a certain amount of income in a tax year before starting to pay tax (see page 21):

- A married woman gets the wife's earned income allowance – the same as a single person's allowance. It can be used to reduce the tax paid on earned income (wages or salary from a job), profit from being self-employed, or pensions paid as a result of the wife's employment or National Insurance contributions. But it *can't* be used to reduce tax on any investment income the wife has: that is counted as the husband's income. In the tax year in which you get married the wife just gets the normal single person's allowance and can use this allowance to set against both her earned and her investment income.

■ A married man gets the married man's allowance – over half as much again as the single person's allowance. It can be set against his own income, his wife's investment income and any of her earned income not covered by her own allowances. In the tax year in which a couple gets married they get the full allowance only if they marry before 6 May. After this they will lose one-twelfth of the difference between the married man's allowance and the single person's allowance for each month they are not married.

So a married couple get a bigger total tax-free allowance between them than two single people, and in turn this usually means less tax to pay (£370 less in the 1987–88 tax year). But this is not always true and a married couple's tax bill may be higher in the following circumstances:

■ If as a married couple they would be paying higher-rate tax (see page 24). Because a married couple's income is lumped together, they start paying higher-rate tax at a much lower joint income than do two single people. You can get round this by having your earnings taxed separately, but if you do this at too low an income, you will end up paying *more* tax – see below.

■ If a married woman has investment income but doesn't have enough earned income to use up her tax-free allowance. This is because she can't use her tax-free allowance to reduce her tax bill as her investment income is always taxed as if it was her husband's. There's no way round this problem (except separation or divorce).

Separate taxation of wife's earnings

With separate taxation the amount of tax-free allowances a couple gets is reduced. Instead of getting the married man's allowance and wife's earned income allowance, each partner gets the single person's allowance. But they double the amount of income they can have before starting to pay higher-rate tax. In the 1987–88 tax year you lose £1,370 in allowances, but your taxable income can be £17,900 *each* before you have to pay higher-rate tax. So you have to balance one against the other.

It is important to get the calculations right or you could end up paying more tax. You'll find full details in the *Which? Tax Saving Guide* (in most libraries), but there are some general rules. There is no point in doing it until you are paying higher-rate tax . And even then whether it is worth while depends on your combined income and how much income the less-well-off partner has. (Remember, you must look at only the wife's *earnings*, as her investment income will always be taxed as if it was her husband's.) The 'break-even' points for 1987–88 are given in Table 1 on page 24.

You can choose to have your earnings taxed separately ('opt for the wife's earnings election') at any time up to a year after the end of the tax year. So for the 1987–88 tax year you must decide before 5 April 1989.

Separate assessment

Do not confuse this with separate taxation – it doesn't affect the total tax bill. Instead it makes the husband and wife each responsible for filling in their own tax return and paying their own tax. You get your normal allowances but these are split between the two of you in proportion to your income.

Who stays at home?

If both partners in a marriage can earn similar amounts but decide that only one will work – perhaps so that the other can look after the home and the children – they will be better off if the woman goes out to work. This is because she will be able to get both the wife's earned income allowance *and* her husband's allowance to set against her earnings. If the husband earns and the wife does not, her allowance can't be transferred to him.

Social security benefits

For the purposes of claiming many benefits, being married

makes no difference at all to what you get. It is important only for contributory benefits (e.g. unemployment benefit and State retirement pensions) which depend on how many National Insurance contributions you have paid: if you are married you may be able to claim extra benefit for your partner (though often only if he or she earns less than a certain amount).

More information

IR31 Income tax and married couples
IR13 Income tax – wife's earnings election
(Both available from your local tax office)

UNMARRIED COUPLES

If you are living together your financial position as regards tax, benefits and so on is not the same as it would be if you were married.

Your tax

Unlike married couples, each partner is responsible for his or her own tax affairs. The Inland Revenue will correspond with you as two separate people and is not concerned with you as a couple.

Where allowances are concerned this means that each of you gets the single person's allowance (see page 22). And each of you can have a large amount of taxable income taxed at the basic rate before starting to pay higher rates. If you have a child living with you who is under 16, or is still in full-time education or training, you can claim the additional personal allowance as well. This brings your total tax-free personal allowances up to the level of the married man's allowance. If you and your partner have at least two children you can each claim this allowance so that you get the equivalent of two married man's allowances.

If one of you doesn't have enough income to make full use of his or her allowance you can't transfer the unused tax-free part to your partner. But your partner can agree to covenant payments to you to make sure that you have enough income to use your allowances (see page 27). The partner making the payments then avoids having to pay tax on the amount covenanted and the partner receiving them will not have to pay any tax. The tax saving can be substantial: up to £1,025 in the 1987–88 tax year.

Another way to use up personal allowances, if you have a child or children, is to arrange an affiliation order from the man to the woman (as long as he is the father of the child). The mother has to apply to her local magistrates court, usually before the child is three; the father then gets tax relief on the amount he is ordered to pay, and it counts as the mother's income so she can set her allowances against it.

Social security benefits

Unmarried couples lose out a little when claiming contributory benefits (see above). You can claim extra for your partner only if he or she is financially dependent on you *and* is looking after your child. And you can't claim a retirement pension or get widow's benefits based on your partner's contributions.

With means-tested benefits, (e.g. supplementary benefit) it is the income and circumstances of the whole household that is taken into account. So an unmarried couple is treated just the same as a married couple (but only if they are of different sexes: same-sex couples are never treated as a couple for social security purposes no matter how close their relationship).

More information

IR29 Income tax and one-parent families
(Available from your local tax office)
NI247 Social Security: Living together as man and wife
(Available from your local DHSS office)

ENDING RELATIONSHIPS

When a relationship comes to an end there are lots of problems and not all of them are financial. But the money matters are particularly important, not least because the same income has to be stretched over two homes.

Emergency help

If you are left on your own with little or no money, you need immediate help to make sure that you keep a roof over your head. Below are a few tips – for more details get advice immediately from a CAB or other advice agency:

- If you are married and live in a rented home you will normally have the right to take over the tenancy even if it was in your spouse's name only. Make sure you continue to pay the rent – you may be able to claim housing benefit to help with the costs – see page 72.

- If you are not married and live in a rented home you have the right to stay only if your name is on the tenancy agreement. If it is in your partner's name only you will not have the right to stay and can be evicted. If it looks as if this might happen go and talk to the local council to see whether they will rehouse you (they must, if you have children).

- If you have a mortgage, let the lenders know what has happened. If you are married and the home is in your spouse's name only you can ensure that it isn't sold without your permission by registering a charge on it – get advice from your CAB or local housing advice centre.

The next important point is to make sure you have the money to live on:

- You may be able to claim a number of benefits to provide you with some income, and help with your rent and rates (see Chapters 6 and 8 for details). But your needs are likely to be complicated: your local CAB will be able to work out what you can get.

- If your money was kept in a joint account, either partner can draw out all the money and run up an overdraft. Avoid the possibility of this either by closing the joint account and putting the money into two separate accounts, or by agreeing that both of you must sign for withdrawals.

When the situation looks clearer, you can think about sorting out the legal side. If it looks as if your separation is going to be permanent, there is not much point in delaying making claims for maintenance, sorting out what will happen to the family home, who will have custody of children and so on. If you don't have children and both partners work it may be possible to do everything without a solicitor. Where there are children, or one partner is likely to need maintenance, or there are going to be disputes over property, pensions and so on it's advisable to have a solicitor. Your CAB should be able to recommend someone suitable and can also check whether you might be able to get free or cheap help under the legal advice and assistance scheme. (But be careful – if you do get help from legal aid and get money or property as a result of the help, the legal fund can recover from you what has been paid to your solicitor. This can make a big hole in any settlement. Ask your solicitor for details.)

The tax position

If you were married, once you are separated or divorced the tax system treats you as two separate people each responsible for his or her own tax affairs. To establish that you are separated, each partner should write to their tax office (if you haven't had any correspondence with a tax office or don't know where yours is just write to the nearest office listed in the phone book). You will be treated as being separated when:

- you draw up a deed of separation, or
- there's a court order for payment of maintenance, or
- there's a decree of judicial separation, or
- when it appears that the separation is likely to be permanent – in practice that will be when the separation has lasted a year, and the effective date of separation will be backdated a year.

In the tax year in which you separate you can claim the following allowances:

- The husband gets the whole of the married man's allowance (no matter when in the year the separation occurs) to set against his income. In addition, the wife's earnings up to the date of the separation count as his and he can claim the wife's earned income allowance against these. So if she had earned at least as much as the allowance before the separation he can use the whole allowance.
- The wife gets the whole of the single person's allowance to set against her earnings from the date of the separation until the end of the tax year.

From the next tax year you each get the single person's allowance (but see Maintenance, below).

Maintenance

This is money one partner pays to the other, or to children, either during separation or after divorce. It is important to pay maintenance in the correct manner, as it may be possible for one partner to get more money than the other pays out.

There are two sorts of maintenance, voluntary and enforceable:

- Voluntary maintenance means just that – the giver can't be forced to hand over the money whatever has been agreed. The recipient does not have to pay any tax on the money received, and normally the giver can't claim any tax relief on the payments (except that a separated husband can continue to claim the married man's allowance if his wife has very little other income).

- Enforceable payments are made under a court order and the courts can make the giver pay up (it is one of the few debts for which you can still be thrown in gaol). The recipient has to pay tax on the money received if their income is high enough and the giver can claim tax back.

Enforceable payments and the giver

How the giver claims a tax refund, or relief, depends on how much maintenance has to be paid under the court order. If it is below a certain amount the giver simply hands over the full amount and gets tax relief either through his or her PAYE coding or in a tax assessment. The limits for these 'small maintenance payments' are as follows:

- £48 a week (£208 a month) paid for an ex-spouse.
- £25 a week (£108 a month) paid *for* a child under 21.
- £48 a week (£208 a month) paid *to* a child under 21.

If the maintenance is higher than the limits, the giver has to deduct basic-rate tax (see page 24) before paying the maintenance. In the 1987–88 tax year this means that for every £100 of maintenance that has to be paid you hand over only £73. As long as you pay at least as much tax in a year as you withhold from the maintenance you can keep the difference. If you pay less, the Inland Revenue will want some of it back. A higher-rate taxpayer can claim tax relief at his or her highest rate of tax and will get the higher-rate tax relief through the PAYE system, or in a tax assessment.

Enforceable payments and the recipient

If the amounts payable under the court order are low enough to count as small maintenance payments (see above), what you get counts as your income and is taxable. But if your total income (including the maintenance you get) is less than your tax-free allowances you won't have any tax to pay.

With larger amounts of maintenance the giver will already have deducted basic-rate tax. So you will not have any more to pay unless your income (including the figure for maintenance before the giver deducted tax – the gross amount) is large enough for you to have to pay higher-rate tax. On the other hand, if your income (including the gross amount of maintenance) is less than your tax-free allowance, you can claim all of the tax back. You will also get a rebate if the amount of tax deducted by the giver is higher than your total tax bill for the year.

Voluntary or enforceable?

Enforceable payments are almost always better both from the tax angle and because the recipient can ensure they get the money they need. Financially one of the only exceptions is where the recipient's top rate of tax is higher than the giver's top rate of tax. Here voluntary payments are better for the couple as a whole as otherwise the recipient will have to pay more tax on the payments than the giver gets in tax relief.

Children and maintenance

All children are entitled to the single person's tax-free allowance (see page 22). When a marriage breaks up it is likely that the partner who looks after the children most of the time will get maintenance for them from the other. If the court order is worded so that this maintenance is paid *to* the child it will count as the child's income so that his or her personal allowance can be used. If the order is worded so that the maintenance is paid *for* the children it becomes the income of the person who receives the money, usually the mother or father, so there may be tax to pay on it. (It doesn't matter if the money is actually paid to the mother or father – what is important is how the court order is worded.)

Divorce and your home

Though you can divide up most possessions on separation or divorce, you can't easily split your home in two. If you own your own home, there are various options:

- The partner who is staying in the home buys out the other. He or she could do this either by forgoing the right to maintenance in return for a lump sum (i.e. a share in the home) or by increasing the mortgage and paying over a lump sum. Either way this could leave you short of money but could be worth considering if you have a good income of your own.

- You agree to sell the home at a later date – perhaps when the children have left school. Until then the partner who moves out agrees to pay all or some of the mortgage. This leaves the partner in the home with more income but means the other is tied to you for a long time.

- You agree to sell the home now and split what is left after the mortgage has been repaid. This may seem the fairest arrangement but what really matters is whether you will be able to afford another home or mortgage.

A married couple can have tax relief on only £30,000 of loans to buy only one home. If you are divorced or separated and are paying the mortgage on your own home and on a home for your ex-spouse you can get tax relief on *both* loans but still only up to a maximum of £30,000 in total. But if you and your ex-spouse each has your own mortgage you can each have tax relief on £30,000 of loans. It is therefore much better to pay maintenance to your ex-spouse, out of which he or she will make their own mortgage repayments. For more on tax relief see page 81.

Financial help from the state

If you are bringing up a child (or children) on your own, you can claim one-parent benefit which will be paid along with your child benefit (see page 111). You can also get an extra tax-free allowance – an additional personal allowance (see page 22) – which brings your total allowances up to the same level as those for a married man.

More information

IR30 *Income tax – separation and divorce*
IR29 *Income tax and one-parent families*
(Both available from your local tax office)

DEATH OF YOUR PARTNER

As well as the obvious emotional problems caused by the death of your partner, you may have money problems. Most of the State help available is for widows. But information in other chapters may help, particularly in Chapters 6 and 11.

Help for widows

Widows can claim special social security benefits and tax allowances.

Benefits

If you are under 60 when your husband dies (or over 60 but he was not getting retirement pension) you get widow's allowance for the first 26 weeks. This is £55.35 a week and you can get £8.05 for each child for whom you also get child benefit. After this you will get one of the following:

- Widowed mother's allowance if you have at least one child under 19. This is £39.50 a week, plus £8.05 for each child, paid until your youngest child reaches 19.

- Widow's pension if you have no children but were 40 or over when your husband died. How much you get depends on your age when he died: £39.50 a week if you were 50 or more, £36.74 if you were 49 and so on down to £11.85 if you were 40.

If you are 60 or more you will get a retirement pension based either on your own contributions, or on those of your husband, or both.

After April 1988 it is proposed that widow's allowance will not be available; instead all widows will get a £1,000 lump sum.

All widow's benefits are taxable except extra amounts paid for children.

Tax

In the tax year in which her husband dies, income up to the date of the death gets the full married man's and full wife's earned income allowance set against it. For her income in the rest of the tax year the widow gets the full single person's tax allowance and the widow's bereavement allowance. She also gets this extra allowance in the following tax year. See page 22 for details of allowances.

Help for widowers

In the tax year in which his wife dies a man gets the full married man's allowance, and can use the wife's earned income allowance to set against his wife's income before she died.

Other financial assistance

If you have to pay for the funeral of your partner (or anyone else who is close) you may be able to get help with the cost from the DHSS. You must be getting supplementary benefit, family income supplement or housing benefit in order to claim and there must be no other way of paying for the funeral, e.g. from money belonging to the person who died or from insurance policies, charities or other relatives. And you must use any savings over £500 first. There are strict rules on what you can claim for – a simple funeral with a plain coffin, fees for the undertaker, chaplain, flowers and so on.

You must apply within three months of the date of the funeral.

More information

NP35 Your benefit as a widow for the first 26 weeks
NP36 Your benefit as a widow after the first 26 weeks
FB29 Help when someone dies
D49 What to do after a death
(All available from your local DHSS)
IR45 What happens when someone dies
IR21 Income tax and widows
(Both available from your local tax office)

11. Children

This chapter looks at the special financial deals for couples and single parents who have children – from the state help available to a woman when she is pregnant to the costs involved in supporting a child through further education.

But the benefits available may not go very far towards the extra costs involved – it might surprise you to find that the total cost of bringing up a child can easily be £75,000. As well as the obvious costs – food, clothes, toys, holidays, school trips, driving lessons and so on – there are less obvious ways in which you spend money on your children.

Typically, both partners will have been earning before their first child is born, but afterwards it is likely there will be only one salary. So the loss of a salary is a cost – as, alternatively, is the cost of paying for someone to look after children if both partners do go out to work. Not only that – at the same time as the income drops, the expenses rise. If you are planning to have children and expect your income to drop, be particularly careful about committing yourself to a large mortgage and other credit agreements that can't be met on one salary. That could lead to a great deal of financial insecurity and problems at the same time as you have the emotional and practical problems involved in bringing up a baby.

A single person having a baby can face even more serious problems. If you have been working you will have to give up work for a period and if you then return to work you will almost certainly need to pay for child care. If you decide to give up work for a longer period the chances are that you will claim benefits – and will probably find that you have to reduce your standard of living quite considerably.

FINANCIAL HELP FROM THE STATE

All women get free prescriptions and dental treatment when
they are pregnant and for the following year. This is the only
help all families can claim before a baby is born – the other state
help is only for working women and those on low incomes.
Once the baby is born anyone can claim child benefit and there
is extra help for single parents and those on low incomes.

Before a baby is born

Many working women will get some financial help when they
give up work to have a baby in the form of statutory maternity
pay (SMP) paid through employers. And some women have the
right to have well over six months maternity leave after the birth
of their baby and still return to their old job. Full details of these
rights are given in Chapter 4.

But some women will not have worked for their current
employer for long enough to get SMP – they, along with self-
employed women and those claiming unemployment benefit,
may be able to get maternity allowance instead.

Maternity allowance

To get this you have to have paid National Insurance contributions for at least 26 out of the 52 weeks ending in the fifteenth
week before your baby is due. Both employed and self-
employed women can claim, though if you pay reduced rate
contributions (see page 132) you are not eligible.

To get the full 18 weeks' worth of allowance, you can stop
work at any time from the end of the twelfth week before the
week in which the baby is due to the end of the seventh week
before. If you stop any later, you will get less than 18 weeks.
You will get £30.05 a week and may be able to claim £18.60 a
week for your husband or for someone looking after a child of
yours. Maternity allowance is not taxable.

Maternity payments

If you are claiming supplementary benefit (see page 61) or
family income supplement (see page 41) you can claim a
maternity payment of £80 from the DHSS to help with the cost
involved when you have a new baby. But there are limits on

how much you can have in savings and still claim. The limit is £500, but if you have less than £80 over the limit, you will get the difference; e.g. if you have £530 in savings, your grant will be £80 less the £30 by which your savings exceed £500, – that is, £50.

Ask your local DHSS for a claim form and return it any time from the eleventh week before the baby is due up until three months after he or she is born.

Free milk and vitamins

If you are getting supplementary benefit or family income supplement you can claim tokens from the DHSS to pay for seven pints of milk a week (worth around £1.75 a week) and vitamin tablets as soon as you know you are pregnant. You can also get them if you are on a low income.

Once the baby is born

Child benefit

This is a weekly payment which can be claimed as soon as a child is born. You can get child benefit for each child until he or she is 16 (or 19 if a student studying up to A-level standard). In 1987–88 child benefit is worth £7.25 a week and is tax-free.

Ask the DHSS for a claim form and fill it in as soon as your baby is born.

One-parent benefit

If you are bringing up a child on your own you can claim an extra £4.70 a week paid along with your child benefit. But you can only get one payment no matter how many children you have. And it will stop if you get married or if you live with someone as husband and wife. (If you are unmarried and have at least one child you can also claim an extra tax-free allowance – the additional personal allowance – see page 22.)

Help if you are on a low income

If you or your partner is working full-time but earns a relatively low amount you may get family income supplement (until April 1988), or family credit (from April 1988) – see page 41. If you or your partner work part-time you may get supplementary benefit (until April 1988), or income support (from April 1988) – see page 61. If you do (and sometimes in other circumstances) you will also get the following:

- Free prescriptions and dental treatment. Also available for all mothers with a baby under 1 year old, children up to the age of 16 and for anyone whose income is low (including children over 16: their parents' income doesn't matter).
- Free milk and vitamins for children until they are 5. These are also available if the family is on a low income.
- Vouchers to help with the cost of glasses. Also available for families on low incomes.
- Free school meals (not available, whatever your circumstances, after April 1988).

Educational maintenance allowance

This is a weekly allowance for children from low-income families who stay on at school after 16. Contact your local education authority to see if you might qualify – each has its own scheme.

More information

FB8 Babies and benefit
NI17A Maternity benefits
CH1 Child benefit
CH11 One parent benefit
FB27 Bringing up children?
FIS1 Family Income Supplement
MV11 Free milk and vitamins
P11 NHS prescriptions
D11 NHS dental treatment
G11 NHS vouchers for glasses
(All available from your local DHSS or CAB)
IR29 Income tax and one-parent families
(Available from your local tax office)

WORKING WHEN YOU HAVE CHILDREN

Whether you are going back to your old job having had maternity leave or going to a new job, the most important thing you must do is make arrangements for your baby to be looked after.

A few firms provide a nursery or crèche. If you do not have to pay anything towards the cost of the service or if you pay less than the full cost you may have to pay some tax on this perk. What you are taxed on is how much it costs your employer, less anything you pay. But if you don't count as higher-paid (broadly if you earn less than £8,500 a year; but see page 33) you will not pay any tax on the perk.

The majority of parents have to make their own arrangements for childcare. Your local authority social services department will be able to give you lists of day nurseries and registered childminders. The other option (usually the most expensive) is to get a nanny – though you may be able to share a nanny with a friend and so reduce the cost.

No matter what sort of childcare you pay for (or how much it costs) you will not be able to count it as a work expense in order to reduce your tax bill, whether you are employed or self- employed.

EDUCATING YOUR CHILDREN

Although state schools are free there are all sorts of extras that parents have to pay for – uniforms, extra-curricular activities such as music lessons and school trips, school meals and so on. But if you want your child to go to a private school it's likely to cost you a lot more. The fees for a prep school could easily be £2,000 or £3,000 a year; boarding school for an older child could cost £5,000 or £6,000. And these are simply the fees – again you have to add on the cost of uniform (which could easily be £300 or even more for a child at prep school) and the other activities.

How to pay school fees

The first thing to check is whether anyone else will pay them! The government's 'assisted places scheme' is designed to help parents of academically able children who want to send their children to private schools but can't afford the fees. Most of the places are for children coming up to the ages of 11 or 13 (though some are kept for students about to start their A-level courses). Before a place is given your child will have to take a written test and have an interview. If the outcome is successful, you will make a contribution to the cost of the fees which will depend on your income.

If your child is particularly bright – either generally or in a specialist field such as music or languages – a private school might have scholarships or 'exhibitions' available which will reduce the costs. Find out about these as early as possible even if it means writing to several schools to see if they have anything which might suit your child. There will usually be a lot of competition and the financial value of the award will not necessarily be high.

Grandparents frequently help pay the costs of their grand-children's education. They can make their help worth around a third more than they actually give by covenanting income to the grandchildren. See page 27 for details.

Parents who can't get help in either of these ways will have to bear the costs of private schooling themselves. Many families struggle financially in order to pay the fees. But if you are thinking ahead you may be able to spread the cost by planning and saving.

The first rule is that it is never too early to start saving for school fees. The second is that whatever scheme you are offered, think carefully about it and what you are committing yourself to, get professional advice and look at the alternative ways of saving for the future (Chapters 14 and 15 might help with this).

There are investment schemes available which are designed to provide money for school fees. Some schemes ask you to invest a lump sum – how much depends on how long it will be invested before you want to start drawing on it to pay fees; with others you invest a regular amount, monthly or annually. With many of these schemes your money is used to buy a series of life insurance policies which are timed to pay out each year so that you can pay the school fees.

If you are thinking of saving for school fees there are two important points to bear in mind:

- Do not over-commit yourself. You can always increase a regular commitment later but you won't necessarily be able to reduce it. Before agreeing to a plan find out what will happen if you could not afford to keep it up. Also check whether the money *has* to be used to pay school fees – you may change your mind about sending your children to private school.

- Do not rely too heavily on a plan. Few plans guarantee that you will get enough money to be able to pay the school fees but will simply pay out money at regular intervals. When the plan is set up all sorts of assumptions will have to be made: how much the insurance company will make on its investments; how fast school fees will increase; what tax rates will be; and so on. If any of these assumptions turns out to be wrong (which is, after all, quite likely) you could end up with more than you need to pay fees, or less.

For information on school fees and details on the various investment plans available, get in touch with the Independent Schools Information Service (ISIS), 56 Buckingham Gate, London SW1E 6AG.

Further education

Even if you haven't had to pay for your child to go to private school you may well find yourself digging into your pocket when the time comes for further education. Although grants are widely available, what you get depends on the family's income – the higher your income, the larger the amount you are expected to contribute to the costs.

Some courses are labelled as 'designated' and attract mandatory grants; that is, the local education authority (LEA) has no choice over whether to pay a grant or not. Broadly if a student is doing a degree course, a teacher training course, an HND or any other course at an equivalent level to these, he or she will get a grant.

How much grant a student gets from the LEA depends on:

- the level of basic grant awarded;
- the family's income and circumstances.

The basic grant is fixed by the Department of Education and is designed to cover a student's basic living, travel and academic expenses both for the three terms and the Christmas and Easter breaks. It varies according to where a student lives and studies: it is highest for a student at college in London and in rented accommodation; lowest for students at college outside London who are living at home with their parents. If the family's income (after making allowances for the number of dependants you have and for other outgoings such as your mortgage) is above a certain amount you will be expected to pay part of the grant and the amount paid by the LEA will be lower. The higher your income, the higher your contributions. Above a certain level there will be no LEA basic grant. Tuition fees are separate and will be paid for even if you do not get any basic grant.

There is full information on grants in a booklet 'Grants for students' which you can get from your LEA. Reading it carefully should give you all the information you need – if you have any queries the LEA will be able to help. You will have to fill in a form detailing your circumstances and the LEA will calculate the grant – it is always worth checking the result. A few points are worth noting:

- Even if it looks as if your income is too high for your child to get a grant you should still apply for one as then the LEA will pay the fees. If you don't apply you will pay them.
- If you have two children at college at the same time, any contribution you have to make isn't doubled but simply split between them. So if the two children are close in age it may be worth the older deferring going to college for a year or so.
- If a student's parents are divorced or separated the grant will usually be assessed only on the income of the parent who has custody. Even if that parent has remarried or is living with someone only the parent's income counts.

Discretionary grants

If a course is not designated it is up to the LEA whether or not to give a grant. There are few rules for whether or not discretionary grants are available for a particular course so it is worth contacting your LEA before even applying for a course to see whether there will be any financial help. For a non-designated advanced course any grant may well be awarded on the same basis as a mandatory grant. But it does all depend on your LEA and its policy. For non-advanced courses such as ONDs or City and Guilds qualifications an LEA may award a small grant but is likely to require that the student lives at home.

Covenants

The best way for parents to make their contributions to a student son or daughter is through a covenant – see page 27.

Other sources of finance

Some companies and employers such as the Forces offer sponsorship to students. In industry these may be 'sandwich' courses where the student is expected to work for the company perhaps for a period in the middle of the course or in the vacations.

Most colleges and universities have scholarships which they award to particularly promising students (though there may also be awards for students coming from a particular town or who have been at a particular school). These awards are unlikely to be worth very much but even a few extra pounds can help students as the basic grant levels are relatively low.

Social security benefits may also help, but the opportunities for claiming are few. Students living in ordinary rented accommodation can apply for housing benefit (see page 72) to help pay their rent and rates. During the Easter and Christmas breaks most students can't claim supplementary or unemployment benefits as their grant is supposed to cover living expenses over these periods, but they can in the long summer vacation. Advice on benefits can be obtained from the welfare officer of the students' union or the local CAB.

More information

Information on assisted places at independent schools is available from the Department of Education and Science, Room 3/65, Elizabeth House, York Road, London SE1 7PH
Grants to students
(Available from the Department of Education and Science, as above, or from your LEA)
IR47 Deed of covenant by parent to adult student
IR59 Students' tax information pack
(Both available from your local tax office)
FB23 Young people's guide to social security
FB20 Leaving school?
(Both available from your local DHSS)

12. Financial protection for you and your family

This chapter is about protecting yourself and those who depend on you against the possibility of hardship in the future. Insurance is a large part of the story – insurance to provide financial assistance to your family if you die at a time when they are financially dependent on you, and insurance to help pay the bills if you are ill and unable to work for a long period. To help choose an insurance company check the latest report in *Which?* magazine. But making provision for how your money is to be passed on to your dependants – through a carefully-written will and proper tax planning – is also important.

LIFE INSURANCE

The first thing to decide is whether you need life insurance. The general rule is that you should take out life insurance if there is anyone who would be worse off as a result of your death. If you are a single and have no dependants then it is not so important. But even so it can be worth while – for example, if you know that you are likely to have dependants in the near future. And the younger you are the less it will cost.

If you are earning it is obvious that if you die your family will be worse off. But it may be less obvious if you are not earning. Here you have to consider how what you do would be replaced. For instance, if you are at home looking after children, think how much it would cost your partner to employ a nanny and someone to run the house. And if you are caring for an elderly or disabled relative, replacement care could well be costly.

How much to insure for

You can't work out the answer to the nearest £1 or even £100, but you can have a good attempt. There are two parts to this:

- How much money will your dependants need so that they will not be worse off after your death – or at the very least so that they will be able to afford the basics of life even if their standard of living is reduced?
- How long will they need this money for?

If you were to die, in the short term your family will need to pay for a funeral (the cost could easily be close to £1,000) and there may be other bills, perhaps including unpaid tax. But it is their longer-term needs that are particularly important. You need to look at how much income would be lost on your death and how much would be gained; and at what extra expenses or reduced expenses there might be. Income that would be lost includes your earnings but could also be maintenance payments. Income that might be gained includes a widow's or widower's pension from your job, or widow's benefits from the State. Extra expenses could be the cost of paying for someone to look after the children and the home; reduced expenses could be the mortgage payments (if you already have life insurance covering your mortgage) and the cost of running a second car. You may already have some life insurance cover – through your job, your mortgage or an investment-type policy – but it may not be enough; an additional term insurance policy would be the cheapest way of topping it up.

The main factors which determine the length of time your family needs the money from insurance will be things such as the ages of your children or of your partner or of any elderly or disabled relative you look after or support financially. For instance if your children are young you might feel you want to provide for them for 15 or 20 years.

Before simply multiplying the annual income required by the number of years, you should consider the effect that inflation will have on the buying power of a given sum of money. For instance, if inflation runs at 5% a year, the value of money halves in as little as 15 years.

Which type of insurance?

There are two basic and very different types of life insurance:

- Pure insurance policies which will pay out a certain sum of money if you die within a given number of years – referred to as 'term' or 'protection-only' insurance. If you outlive your chosen number of years (called the 'term' of the policy) you get nothing.

■ Insurance policies which combine life insurance with savings and pay out a lump sum at the end of a fixed period or when you die. A lot of these investment-type life insurance schemes are called 'endowment' policies, but there are other sorts too.

Term insurance is the cheapest form of protection, so if you simply want to provide for your dependants it will be the best choice for you. Investment policies put your protection and savings plans in one basket: you may be better keeping these two important features of your financial planning separate – you have more flexibility and may be able to invest in more suitable investments (see Chapter 15).

Term insurance

There are two different sorts of policy. One pays out a lump sum (which could be invested by your dependants to provide an income), the other pays a regular income. With a lump sum policy your dependants will get the same amount whether you die two years into the term of the policy or in its last year. A family income benefit policy, though, pays income only from the time of your death until the end of the term. So if you died towards the end of the term the income would be paid for a few years only. You can of course choose to take out two (or more) policies, one a lump sum policy and one a family income benefit policy.

There are all sorts of features which may be added at extra cost to a simple policy of either sort. To help cope with inflation, you can buy policies which increase the amount of cover as the years go by, either increasing it by a fixed amount or along with inflation. For many people one of these escalating policies will be the best choice, although you could simply take a guess at what you expect inflation to be and buy a simple, level policy. Some term insurances give the option of converting your policy into an investment-type one or allowing you to increase the amount of insurance every five years. You may not need or want this flexibility – if you don't you will be wasting your money.

Joint life policies are available for couples and may be slightly cheaper than two separate policies. The policy will pay out on the first death and then the cover comes to an end. Partly because of this and partly with the problems that could arise if you and your partner split up, it may well be wise to get two separate policies.

You can buy insurance policies where the amount of insurance reduces as the years go by. These are designed to pay off a loan, such as a mortgage, that you are repaying over a long period and are often called 'mortgage protection' policies. If money is very tight, as it often is when you buy your first home, such a policy can be a good way of ensuring that your mortgage will be paid off if you die. But if you can afford it, a level term policy could be a better choice.

Self-employed people or employees who have some freelance earnings or who are not members of their employer's pension scheme can get full tax relief on their life insurance premiums. This means that each £10 premium will cost only £7.30 – a worthwhile saving. If you are in this position you will need to ask for quotes for Section 226A life insurance. There is a limit on the amount of your earnings you can pay in premiums on Section 226A policies and to personal pension plans – see page 139.

You usually pay for insurance in monthly instalments called 'premiums'. The main factors affecting how much the premium will be are as follows:

- How much do you want the policy to pay out if you die? In general, the premiums for a policy which pays out, say, £50,000 will be getting on for twice as much as for a policy which pays out £25,000.

- How long is the term? The longer the term, the greater the chance that you will die before the end of it so the higher the premium you have to pay.

- How old are you? The older you are, the greater the chance that you will die within the term of the policy so the higher the premium. For instance, the premium for someone aged 39 could be two-and-a-quarter times that of the premium for someone aged 29, and if you are 44 you could pay one-and-three-quarters as much as a 39-year-old. So waiting just a few years before buying life insurance can mean much larger premiums.

- What is your sex? Women live longer than men so,

for example, the chance of a women of 30 dying in the next 20 years is lower than it is for a man of 30. Consequently, premiums for women are lower than for men of the same age.

Investment policies

These may appear to be a better deal than insurance-only policies as they guarantee to pay out at some time whether you die within the term or not. As well as providing life insurance your premiums are invested by the insurance company and what you get at the end of the policy (or when you die) depends on how well the investments have fared. But there are several drawbacks:

- They are more expensive than term policies.
- They tie up your savings for a long time and if you need your money out before the end of the set time you could lose out.
- You may get a better deal from another sort of investment.

There are three main types of policy:

- With an endowment policy you pay premiums for a set number of years – 15, 20 and so on. At the end of this period (or on your death) the policy will pay out. A non-profit endowment policy guarantees to pay out a set amount. These are generally regarded as bad value for money. A with-profits endowment policy also guarantees a set amount but over the years this amount is increased as the company adds 'bonuses'. You can't predict what the bonuses are going to be worth – any projections are done in a standard way by the insurance company and how well they have done in the past is no guide as to how they will perform in the future. And what sounds like a large sum now could be worth a lot less in 20 years' time simply as a result of inflation.
- Whole life policies are just that – they last for the rest of your life and pay out only when you die. With some policies you have to pay the premiums until you die too; others allow you to stop when you get to a certain age. The policies are similar to with-profits endowment policies in that the value of your investment grows over the years as bonuses are added. A whole life policy can be useful if you're worried about how your heirs are going to pay inheritance tax on what you leave – see page 128.

- With unit-linked policies, part of your premium goes to provide life insurance, and the rest is invested by the insurance company. What you get back when you die or at the end of the policy depends on how well the investment is doing at that time – its value can go down as well as up. So this is a riskier way of saving than a straightforward endowment policy.

INSURANCE AGAINST ILLNESS

Illness is worrying enough, without having to cope with the additional financial burdens. Two types of insurance might help: permanent health insurance, to help pay the household bills if you are too ill to work; and private patients insurance to give you private hospital treatment if you want it.

Permanent health insurance

Insurance which pays an income if you are ill is not always necessary: check first what you are entitled to already. If you are employed find out how much sick pay you would get from your employer and for how long. Some generous employers will pay your full salary until you are able to return to work, others pay for only a few months, and some pay nothing in excess of State benefits (see page 35). If you are self-employed there will be no employer to help, so you would have to rely on your savings and state benefits. If you do not work outside the home there would be no help from the State unless you are ill for a long time – and you might find yourself having to paying extra bills, for example for a childminder or for someone to look after an elderly or disabled relative for you.

How health insurance works

In return for a regular premium you get a monthly income while you are ill and unable to work. Many policies will also continue to pay out to top-up your income when you return to work if as a result of your illness you have to do a lower-paid job or if you can work only part-time. Once you've taken out a policy it will last as long as you continue to pay the premiums – the company can't cancel it just because you make very long or frequent claims.

How much it costs

This depends on several factors:

- How much income you want the policy to pay out. This is for you to choose but companies will not usually let you take out a policy that pays more than three-quarters of your normal earnings. And if you have no earnings there will be a limit on what the policy will pay out, perhaps as little as £50 a week. Whatever level of cover you choose, don't forget the effect of inflation; otherwise what seems like a large monthly income now could be worth a relatively small amount if it is a long time before you claim or if you are ill for a long period. A policy which increases the cover before you claim and which increases the income it pays out during a claim is probably the best (though most expensive) type to choose.

- How long you wait after you become ill before the policy starts to pay an income. There is always a delay – no policy will pay as soon as you become ill. The shortest waiting (or 'deferment') period is usually four weeks, though with a few companies it is three months. At the other end of the scale you can choose to wait as long as one year. The longer the waiting period, the lower the premium. When deciding what is best for you, look at what other income you get. For instance, if your employer pays you full pay for three months and half pay for another three you may decide it's worth having a six-month waiting period.

- Your sex. Women usually have to pay around half as much again as men because insurance companies claim that women are ill more often and for longer periods than men.

- Your age. In general, the older you are at the start of the policy, the higher the premium.

- Your job. The more likely you are to be off work as a result of your job, the higher the premium. A teacher or secretary would be in the lowest 'risk' group, a salesman would be in the higher risk group and a builder in the highest risk group.

- Your health. If you have been ill a lot, or if there is a history of illness in your family, your premium could be higher. In some cases you could be refused cover. On the other hand, some policies offer discounts to non-smokers.

PRIVATE PATIENTS INSURANCE

Although many people are quite happy with the care they get from the National Health Service (NHS), others prefer to pay for their own treatment. That can be very expensive (from £1,750 to £3,500 for a hip replacement operation), so several groups offer insurance to cover the bills.

There may be advantages to private health treatment – those frequently quoted are as follows:

■ Fewer delays. The NHS will respond very quickly if emergency or urgent treatment is needed, but there are long waiting lists for many non-urgent operations and consultations. Opting for private treatment is likely to reduce the time you have to wait for non-urgent treatment.

■ Treatment timed to your needs. With the NHS you are not likely to have much choice about when you go to see consultants or go into hospital. Private treatment is more likely to give you appointments that suit you.

■ More privacy. You will almost certainly get a private room if you pay for your own treatment. In an NHS hospital you are likely to have to be in a ward – though usually sharing with no more than ten others.

It is up to you to decide whether these factors are important. If you are self-employed you may find the idea of having choice over when you go into hospital appealing as you could choose a time when business was slack. On the other hand you may not like the idea of being in a room on your own, preferring to be in a ward with others to chat to.

The policies

Insurance can pay almost all the bills involved in medical treatment – from consultants' fees and X-rays, through surgeons' and anaesthetists' fees, to nursing at home during convalescence. But there will be limits. Most policies restrict the total you can claim each year to perhaps £50,000. Others limit the amounts that can be paid out for the various parts of your treatment – perhaps £300 for an operation such as having your tonsils out, £650 for a major operation such as a hip replacement, and £400 for a course of radiotherapy.

When choosing a policy, look out for what is *not* covered. Policies will usually not pay out for treatment if the problem existed before you took out the policy (unless you gave full details on your application form). Other exclusions could include any costs involved in normal pregnancy and childbirth (though complications may be covered); the cost of being in a nursing home or hospital through old age; illness which is a result of drug or alcohol abuse; treatment of psychiatric problems; or kidney dialysis.

The cost

This depends on the following:

- Your age and that of anyone else on the policy. The younger you are, the cheaper the premium. But premiums usually increase each year with your age.
- The amount of cover offered by the policy. Some policies offer relatively low amounts of cover in return for lower premiums. The problem is that if you needed a lot of treatment (or very expensive treatment) the amounts allowed could be inadequate. (If you are generally happy to be treated under the NHS but don't want to have to wait for treatment, the type of policy which pays out only if the waiting list for NHS treatment is over six weeks could be good value.)
- The type of hospital you want. Many policies differentiate between types of hospital and charge higher premiums if you opt for treatment in London post-graduate teaching hospitals than if you choose provincial teaching hospitals or provincial non-teaching hospitals.
- Discounts. Lots of discounts are available – these can reduce the cost by anything from 5% to 40%. Depending on the company, you could get a discount for paying by direct debit; if you are a non-smoker; for being a member of the RAC or AA; for paying by credit card; for being a member of a group scheme; or because you are a member of trade or professional association. Some policies even offer no-claims discounts. There are also reductions for accepting an 'excess' – agreeing to pay the first part of each claim yourself.

PASSING YOUR MONEY ON

Everyone should make a will. A properly written will can make things easier for your family and friends, cut down on possible arguments and ensure that your dependants are able to cope financially. Another thing you should do is to see if you can arrange your affairs so as to minimise the inheritance tax that may have to be paid on your money and possessions when you die.

Your will

If you do not make a will, everything you own is passed to your family according to the intestacy rules. The rules are complicated (and Scotland and Northern Ireland have their own rules), for instance, if you are married and everything you own is worth less than £40,000 it will all go to your widow or widower. If you are worth more than £40,000 and have children, your widow or widower gets only £40,000 and your personal possessions; the rest is invested and your widow or widower can have half of the interest for the rest of her or his life; your children share the remainder of the interest, and the capital is divided between them when your widow or widower dies. A single person who has no children would find their money going to his or her parents, or if they are dead to his or her brothers and sisters.

Although there is no law to stop you making your own will, it is well worth using a solicitor: the cost is unlikely to be much more than £30 and you will be sure that it has been done properly, in accordance with the rules. But you can make things easier for the solicitor (and possibly keep your bill down) by doing your homework first:

- Make a list of everything you own that needs to be included in your will (if you own your home jointly, your half may pass automatically to the other owner – ask your solicitor for advice on this). Get a rough idea of what everything is worth.

- List the people or charities you want to benefit from your will, including full names and addresses. As you will not know exactly how much you will be worth when you die, it is normal practice to leave specific gifts to certain people and then say who is to get the remainder; that is, the residue.

- Think about who you want to deal with your affairs and carry out the wishes in your will – your executor. You can have more than one (two is normal) and you should always check that they are willing to do the task. Many people choose their husband or wife as one executor and one of their children as the other. In any case it is sensible if at least one of the executors is somewhat younger than you. Your bank or solicitor can act as executor but they will charge for their services and your heirs will get less.

■ Think about inheritance tax (see below) and who will pay it. It is usually paid out of the residue, but you can say that each gift has to bear its own share of the tax.

Inheritance tax

When you die, if the value of what you leave comes to more than a certain amount (£90,000 in 1987–88), inheritance tax is charged on the extra. But anything you leave to your husband or wife or to charities is left out of the count. And anything you owe is deducted from the total. But you can't escape inheritance tax simply by hastily giving things away if you think you are about to die – tax might also be payable on things you give away up to seven years before you die. But there are certain types of gifts which are ignored – these exempt transfers include gifts of up to £3,000 in each tax year, plus gifts:

■ between husband and wife;
■ to registered charities and certain institutions (e.g. National Trust, museums or universities);
■ to political parties (though there is a limit of £100,000 for gifts made on death or in the year before);
■ to people getting married (within certain limits);
■ to help support an elderly or disabled relative;
■ of up to £250 to as many people as you like in a tax year;
■ that you pay out of your income on a regular basis (e.g. covenants to grandchildren).

Keeping the tax bill down

There is quite a lot of scope for keeping the size of an inheritance tax bill down. But it does require careful planning. Here are some points to think about:

■ Before starting to give money away, make sure that you and your partner will have enough to live on in later years. Don't forget the effect of inflation.

- If you do give things away, try to keep your gifts within the rules for tax-exempt gifts.

- If you are married, both you and your spouse can make full use of the exempt gifts. If one has a lot more money than the other, consider transferring money between the two of you so each can make use of exempt gifts. (But you can't make it a condition of a transfer between the two of you that the money or whatever is given away).

- If you leave everything to your husband or wife there will be no tax to pay on your death but when he or she dies the total tax bill could be larger as it will be based on your combined estate.

- Any life insurance policies should be written in trust for a particular person – there is then no inheritance tax payable on the amount paid out on your death. If you have an existing policy you should be able to get it changed – the insurance company will be able to tell you what needs to be done.

- If it looks as if the tax bill when you die will be large or if your heirs will have to sell things they would rather keep in order to pay the tax, think about taking out some life insurance to pay all or some of the tax. Whole life insurance which pays out on your death could be a good choice, but term insurance is much cheaper – see page 121. However, if you are elderly or your health is poor, the premiums will be expensive. Make sure the policy is written in trust (see above).

- If it looks as if your tax bill will be large, get advice from a solicitor or accountant specialising in inheritance tax. Be wary about tax avoidance schemes – do not put any money in one without independent advice.

13. Planning for retirement

This chapter covers the main long-term plan you can – and should – make for your retirement: your pensions. It used to be a simple business: if you were lucky, you got something from your employer; otherwise you relied on what you got from the State. But the possibilities are now wider, and everyone has to make some choices. And from 1988 it is likely that these choices will be much greater, so your task in planning what to do becomes even more complicated.

There is, however, one general rule. Pension schemes – whether run by the State or employers, or by financial groups such as banks or insurance companies – are all basically ways of saving money while you are earning so that you can have an income when you retire. The more you save, and the longer the period you save for, the greater your pension will be. So you can't really start paying into pension schemes too early in your working life.

The following are the main different types of pension discussed in this chapter, and very briefly how they relate to each other. They are explained in detail on the page numbers shown.

- **Basic state retirement pension.** Everyone gets this, at a flat rate each week, if they have paid enough National Insurance contributions (see page 131).
- **Earnings-related state pension.** This gives you extra pension based on earnings: the higher your pay over your working life, the more pension you eventually get. The main scheme is the State Earnings Related Pension Scheme, or SERPS (page 133). If your employers run their own pension scheme (see below) you may or may not get SERPS. In 1988 minimum personal pension plans (page 134) will be introduced. These

are very roughly a privatised version of SERPS: if you are in SERPS, you can choose to swap over or stay as you are. There is also an antiquity: the graduated state pension which operated between 1961 and 1975 (page 135).

- **Occupational pension.** This is provided by your employer, though you usually have to help pay for it too (page 135). It is often earnings-related.
- **Personal pension.** This is a private pension plan you pay for yourself, though employers may contribute (page 139). How much pension you will get depends partly on how much you pay in, so it is not strictly earnings-related (though of course, the more you earn, the more you can afford to pay in; and the amount on which you can get tax relief is fixed as a percentage of your earnings). Self-employed people have been able to take out personal pension plans for many years, as have people in jobs who don't belong to their employer's scheme. From 1988, people in employers' schemes will be able to opt out and take out a personal pension instead.

There is guidance about how to decide which scheme to go for, when you have choices, on page 141.

BASIC STATE PENSION

Most people will get at least some basic retirement pension when they reach pension age (60 for women, 65 for men) though if you don't want it then you can delay getting it for up to five years – when you will get it at a higher rate whether you are still working or not.

To get the full pension you need to have paid National Insurance contributions for most of your working life. This isn't the length of time you actually work before retiring, but the length of time you *could* have worked, usually 44 years for a woman, 49 for a man (can be less for people born before 6 July 1932). If you miss more than a few years you will get a reduced pension.

However, there is some protection for people who actually *can't* pay contributions. People claiming certain benefits including unemployment, sickness, invalidity or maternity benefit, statutory sick or maternity pay, automatically get their National Insurance contributions credited so don't have to worry about their pension entitlement. There is a similar system if you are at home looking after children or someone who is sick or elderly. But this home responsibilities protection has been available only since 1978 and unless you are getting child benefit, you may not automatically get it.

You can make up missed contributions by paying them voluntarily. But before doing this you should ask the DHSS for a statement of your National Insurance record and ask them to tell you how many more contributions you need to pay to get a full pension.

Married women

Reduced rate National Insurance contributions paid by some married women and widows don't count towards a pension. If you are still paying these you should consider whether or not to switch to full-rate contributions. Broadly it may be worth doing in these circumstances:

- If you are older, or less than five years younger, than your husband and will have time to build up a basic pension of your own before you reach 60. Otherwise you will not get any retirement pension until your husband starts drawing his.
- If you are planning to give up work to have a child, as you will then be able to claim home responsibilities protection straight away (otherwise you would have to wait two years before you automatically receive it).

There are other factors to consider – your local DHSS should be able to give you guidance on what is best for you. You can't now opt to pay reduced rate contributions, and if you currently do so and then do not work for two years (or earn too little to pay contributions), or get divorced, you automatically lose the right to pay reduced contributions.

How much?

In the tax year starting April 1987 you will get £39.50 a week. If you are married, each of you can get this much if you have each paid enough National Insurance contributions. A married man will get an extra £23.75 a week for his wife if she isn't entitled to more pension than that on her account or if she is under 60 and doesn't earn more than a certain amount. A woman can't usually claim for her husband (though this may change in the future). If you earn more than £75 a week your pension will be reduced (though not if you are a woman of 65 or more or a man who is 70 or more). The amounts go up each April, normally in line with inflation.

More information

NP27 *Looking after someone at home? How to protect your pension*
NP32 *Your retirement pension*
NP32A *Your retirement pension if you are widowed or divorced*
NP32B *Retirement benefits for married women*
NI1 *Married women – Your National Insurance position*
NI51 *Widows – Guidance about NI contributions and benefits*
NI95 *NI guide for divorced women*
NI196 *Social security benefit rates and earnings rules*
(All available from your local DHSS)

SERPS

You pay for a State Earnings Related Pension with part of your National Insurance contributions; the greater your earnings (and so the greater your National Insurance contributions) the more pension you will get. But working out how much more is very complicated. The only earnings that count are those between the point at which you start to pay National Insurance contributions and the point at which you pay no more contributions (the lower and upper earnings limts – see page 30).

When the scheme was first introduced in 1978 the idea was that when you retired your pension would be calculated by taking one-eightieth of each year's earnings between these points (after taking account of inflation) and adding them all together. If you had been a member of SERPS for more than 20 years, your pension would be based on the best 20 years (after adjusting for inflation), no matter when they were. People retiring before April 1999 will have their SERPS worked out in this way.

But the rules are being changed. If you are due to retire after April 2009 your pension will be based on your average earnings over the whole of your working life – not just the best years. So people who have periods of unemployment or relatively low earnings will get less than they would under the original scheme. And instead of geting a final pension worth one-quarter of revalued earnings it will be only one-fifth. If you are due to retire between April 1999 and April 2009 your SERPS entitlement will be between a quarter and a fifth of revalued earnings.

You have to be employed to benefit from SERPS. Then until minimum personal pension plans are introduced one of the following will apply to you:

- If your firm has no pension scheme you will be contributing to SERPS – you can't choose not to. If you want to build up an extra pension you can also pay into a personal pension plan.

- If your firm has a pension scheme but you're not a member you have to contribute to SERPS. But you can have a personal pension plan as well.

- If you are a member of your firm's pension scheme you may or may not be contributing to SERPS – that depends on whether or not the firm's scheme is 'contracted-out' of SERPS. In either case, you can't also have a personal pension plan unless you have some self-employed or non-pensioned earnings).

MINIMUM PERSONAL PENSION PLANS FOR EMPLOYEES

At its most basic level, a personal pension plan is an alternative, private, SERPS scheme. Instead of the pension portion of your National Insurance contributions going to the State's pension plan, they can be redirected to any commercial pension plan on the market. To make sure you actually *do* contribute to a scheme, the DHSS will make the payments for you out of your National Insurance contributions. But aside from this bit of State control, the scheme works just like investing in any private pension plan – see page 139 for details of how they work.

The scheme will not provide you with a lot of pension because the amount of your National Insurance contribution used, called the National Insurance rebate, is quite small (5.9% of your earnings between the lower and upper earnings limits in 1988–89). And your widow or widower will get only half of the pension earned by your contributions. So you might want to take out additional private pension plans, too, if your employer does not run a scheme. To encourage people to opt out of SERPS, the Government will pay an extra 2% until the 1992–93 tax year.

GRADUATED PENSION

What you get depends on how much you earned between 1961 and 1975. If you earned more than £9 a week at that time you had to pay extra graduated National Insurance contributions. For every £9 of contributions paid a woman would get a pension of just over 5p a week in 1987 – a man would get this much for each £7.50 of contributions. This will rise with inflation but the graduated pension will never make a big contribution to your retirement income.

OCCUPATIONAL PENSION

All schemes work on broadly the same principles. You and your employer contribute to a pension fund and, when you retire, you get an income for the rest of your life. Some schemes include other benefits such as life insurance and pensions for dependants. An employer doesn't have to have a pension scheme but if there is one it has to follow certain rules. These lay down the minimum and maximum benefits which the scheme must provide in order to get the favourable tax treatment which is what makes it worth while to both run and invest in pension plans.

Most schemes ask employees to contribute a small percentage of their pay – often 4% or 5%. You do not have to pay tax on this, so each £100 you pay costs you only £73 (with basic-rate tax at 27%; it is even less if you pay tax at higher than basic rate). Your employer also contributes a percentage of your pay, often two or three times higher than your contribution. The money paid into the pension fund is invested by the trustees of the scheme and the profits made are tax-free. This makes investing in your firm's pension scheme a very tax-efficient way of saving for retirement.

What you get when you retire depends on what sort of pension scheme your employer runs. With a final pay scheme your pension will be based on the amount you were earning in the last few years before you retired (or left the scheme) and how long you had been contributing to the scheme. So you are guaranteed to get a certain amount of pension, and how much you get isn't dependent on how well (or badly) your contributions have been invested over the years. A generous scheme would provide a pension of one-sixtieth of your final pay for each year you contributed. So if you had been a member of the scheme for 40 years your pension would be two-thirds (40/60) of your final pay. A pension of one-eightieth of your final pay for each year you contributed is more common so that 40 years' service would give a pension of half of final earnings after 40 years.

Money purchase schemes are rather different. When you retire, the fund of money that your contributions and those of your employer have grown to are used to buy an annuity (a pension). In this way they are similar to the way personal pensions work, so what you get depends on how good your employer's pension trustees are at making investment choices and what interest rates are like when you retire, rather than directly on how much you have been earning. You could do better or worse than with a final pay scheme.

Links with SERPS

This is where things get really complicated. If your employer's scheme is contracted-out of SERPS both you and your employer pay lower National Insurance contributions. In return, your employer's scheme undertakes to pay a pension at least equivalent to what your SERPS pension would have been – the guaranteed minimum pension (GMP). If your employer's scheme has not contracted-out the benefits it provides will be in addition to SERPS.

Money purchase pension schemes have not in the past been allowed to contract-out, so that employees in such schemes have been sure of getting the SERPS pension as well. From April 1988 money purchase schemes are allowed to contract-out. Instead of having to provide a minimum pension (like contracted-out final pay schemes) there will simply be a minimum contribution – the National Insurance rebate. This means all of your pension (apart from the basic state pension) will depend on factors over which you have no control.

Increasing your pension

If you pay extra contributions to your firm's pension scheme you will be increasing the size of your pension. From October 1987 everyone can make these additional voluntary contributions (AVCs) either into their employer's scheme or a scheme of their choice. You can pay up to a total of 15% of your earnings into your firm's pension scheme and get full tax relief, so if your normal contributions are 5% of your salary you could pay another 10% in AVCs. Before deciding, discuss with your firm's pension adviser or manager what benefits AVCs will buy and compare this with what they will buy in a separate policy.

Changing jobs

People who change employers several times during their career tend to end up with smaller pensions than someone who remains with the same firm all their working life. But legislation is improving the position for so-called 'early leavers'. You may be able to choose to do one of the following:

■ Leave your pension behind. In a final scheme your pension when you retire will be based on your salary when you left the firm. Suppose you worked for a firm for five years when you were young and left thirty years ago when you were earning £650 a year. A pension of one-eightieth of final pay for each year means that your pension from that job will be only five-eightieths of £650 – £41 a year. That doesn't buy a lot now. The position is better for people changing jobs after 1 January 1986 as any pension earned since 1 January 1985 has to be increased by the rate of inflation, or 5% a year, whichever is lower. This will improve the lot of early leavers in final pay schemes. Money purchase schemes are generally better for early leavers as the 'fund' of contributions you leave behind will continue to grow right through until you start to draw your pension. Your employer must allow you to leave your pension contributions invested in the fund if you have been a member of the pension scheme for at least five years (it's planned to reduce this to two years after April 1988).

■ Transfer your pension to your new employer – but only if your new employer's pension scheme allows such transfers (your old employer has no choice over the transfer) and if you have been a member of the scheme for at least five years, or two years from April 1988. In a money purchase scheme the amount transferred is simply the value of your fund; with a final pay scheme the transfer value is related to your final pay and how long you have been contributing. If the new employer's scheme is money purchase your transfer value becomes your new fund; if it is a final pay scheme it will buy you so many years' contributions (almost certainly fewer years than you had in the old scheme).

■ Transfer your pension to an insurance company pension plan. The transfer value of your old plan goes into a money purchase scheme with an insurance company. Such plans are often called 'section 32 buy-out plans'. When you retire the accumulated fund is used to buy a pension.

■ Transfer your pension into a new personal pension. It is planned that you will be able to do this from April 1988. Again it will be a money purchase plan.

■ Withdraw your pension contributions. You can do this only if the scheme allows it and you have been contributing to it for less than five years (less than two years if you leave after April 1988). Even then you can take back only what *you* have put in, not your employer's contributions. Although some tax will be deducted and any interest paid will be low, the tax rules mean that what you get back could be equivalent to a high rate of return on your investment.

Which to choose

It is not easy to decide what to do with your pension rights when you leave a job. Here are a few pointers:

■ Unless you are very young (well under 30) you should not seriously considering withdrawing your contributions.

■ If you have been contributing to a final pay pension scheme for some time, only the pension you have earned since January 1985 will automatically increase with inflation (a maximum of 5% a year). The rest will be frozen unless the trustees of the scheme decide to pay an increase.

■ If you expect to change jobs again you may improve your pension by transferring to an insurance company plan or one of the new personal pension plans.

Whatever you do get advice from the pension advisers of

both your old and new employer before deciding. You will need to compare the benefits of both schemes including such things as how the pension you will get increases (if at all), at what age you can retire, what happens if you have to retire early through ill-health and what pension is provided for dependants such as your widow or widower and children.

More information

How changing jobs affects your pension
(Send s.a.e. to Company Pensions Information Centre, 7 Old Park Lane, London W1Y 3LJ)

PERSONAL PENSION PLANS

If you are self-employed (whether or not you are an employee as well) or if you are not in your employer's pension scheme, you have been able to invest in your own pension plan and get full tax relief on the investment for some years. And it's planned that from April 1988 people already in their employer's scheme can opt out of that and into a personal pension plan instead.

A personal pension is simply a money purchase pension (see page 136) you pay for yourself by putting money in an insurance company plan. Your money is invested by the insurance company and when you want to draw your pension (which need not be at the state pension age) you use the accumulated fund to buy a pension (or you can take a lump sum plus a smaller pension).

One of the most attractive things about pension plans is that you get tax relief on the amount you invest. So each £100 effectively costs you only £73 (with basic rate at 27%; the cost is less if you pay tax at higher than basic rates). There are limits to how much you can invest each year and still get tax relief, depending mainly on your age. The limits below are for the tax year 1987–88.

Year in which you were born	Maximum % of taxable profit
1934 or later	17.5%
1916 to 1933	20%
1914 or 1915	21%
1912 or 1913	24%

Types of personal pension plan

There are three main types of plan. In a 'with-profits' plan the insurance company guarantees that you will get a certain minimum pension, or minimum sum with which to buy a pension. This amount will be quite low, but as the insurance company makes profitable investments it will add 'bonuses' to the guaranteed amounts. So your pension fund grows gradually from the time you take out a policy until you want a pension. (Non-profit policies guarantee a higher amount than a with-profits plan at the outset but this amount does not rise at all. This type of policy is not recommended, though it may be worth considering if you are very close to retirement.)

With a 'unit-linked' plan your contributions buy 'units' in the investment fund or funds of your choice; for example, you might decide you want your money invested in shares and government stocks. The value of your 'units' will go up and down with the total value of the investments in the fund. So how well you do depends very much on when you invest and withdraw. This is more risky, because you can't tell in advance what value your units will have when you want your pension.

A 'deposit administration' plan works much like a bank or building society account in that interest is paid on the balance in your pension fund. It is particularly useful in the last few years before retirement as your premiums are safe and you can be sure that you won't lose anything.

How to choose

You can invest in as many different plans and companies as you want, and spreading your investments between with-profits and unit-linked pension plans with more than one company is a good way of hedging your bets. And as you get close to retirement you could consider a deposit administration-type plan or even a non-profit one.

It is important to do your homework before choosing a pension plan or plans. Don't pick the first plan you are offered – get several quotes from brokers and insurance companies. Don't get taken in by what looks like enormous lump sums and yearly pensions – remember the effects of inflation. Compare the charges too.

More information

Self-Employed Pensions (from *Financial Times* Business Publishing) *Money Management*, and *Planned Savings* are both monthly magazines which publish regular surveys on personal pension plans.

MAKING CHOICES

New legislation planned to come into force during 1988 will mean that you will be able to choose between some of the various types of pension:

- If you are not a member of your employer's pension scheme (or your firm does not have one) you can choose whether to contribute to SERPS or to a new personal pension scheme.
- If you are already a member of your employer's pension scheme you can choose between contributing to that or to a personal pension scheme from April 1988.

SERPS or minimum personal pension?

One of the basic differences is that the pension you get from one of the new plans will depend on how well your contributions have been invested and what interest rates are like when you retire. If your plan doesn't do too well and interest rates are low, your pension could be relatively small. The risk is yours. With SERPS, the Government guarantees that your SERPS pension will be related to your earnings.

It is not possible to say definitely that any particular person will be better, or worse, off staying in SERPS. You would need to be able to predict such things as interest rates, how your earnings will alter between now and retirement, and what annuity rates will be like when you retire. In general, the younger you are the greater are the chances that a personal pension will provide a larger pension than SERPS. Other things you should think about include the following:

- With SERPS, years when you don't pay contributions because you are ill or at home bringing up a family are ignored when calculating your pension, which is good. With personal pensions nothing will go into your plan when you're not working (though your previous contributions will hopefully be increasing in value).

- With SERPS your contributions are worth the same whenever you make them. With a personal pension, the longer your contribution has to grow, the higher the pension it will provide so that each £ invested buys a larger pension for a younger person than for someone older.
- Women generally retire younger so their contributions will have less time to build up in a pension plan than those for men.

In very general terms, men over 40 and women over 35 should think very carefully before opting out of SERPS; even if you are younger than this, it shouldn't be an automatic decision. Don't let the 2% extra from the Government sway you too much either.

Employer's pension or personal pension?

The first step is to find out everything you can about your employer's scheme. Then you have to compare the benefits of this with what you will get by investing a similar amount in a personal pension plan. Think about these points:

- How old you are. The older you are the shorter the time your investment in a personal pension plan will have to grow. Your sex also affects this as women usually retire before men. If you are a man over 40 or a woman over 35 the chances are fairly high that a personal pension plan won't provide a larger pension than a typical final pay scheme.
- Your employer's contribution. This is likely to be a lot larger than the amount *you* pay, so that more money is going to build up your pension – perhaps particularly important for money purchase schemes. If you opt out of your employer's scheme, your employer won't have to pay into your personal pension (apart from the employer's share of the National Insurance rebate).
- How your pension will increase in retirement. Your employer's pension may increase by a generous amount each year (perhaps even be index-linked).
- Early retirement. What will happen if you want to retire early – either by choice or through ill health? Many employers' schemes offer generous terms for ill-health retirement.

■ Your prospects. If your prospects for promotion are good and you expect your salary to rise far ahead of inflation, a final pay scheme could provide a much larger pension than a personal pension plan. But if you intend to wind down as you get older, perhaps working only part time, a personal pension plan might be a better bet.

Think carefully before opting out of your employer's scheme – it may be tempting to opt out and have more spending power by contributing only to a minimum personal plan but you will be reducing your spending power in retirement considerably.

HOW MUCH PENSION WILL YOU NEED?

The further you are away from retiring, the harder this is to quantify, but in general you need to look at what you spend today and try to decide how your spending will differ when your retire. For instance, will you:

■ have finished paying for your mortgage?
■ have larger heating or food bills?
■ take more holidays or be able to cut your expenses by going at cheaper times of the year?
■ need only one car instead of two or will you have to pay for running a car instead of using a company car?

Don't expect to come up with an exact figure – the best you can get is a rough idea. But looking at what you will need is important, particularly if you are due to retire in the next ten years or so as there is still time to invest more in your pension if you find there is a big gap between what you expect to get and what you need.

14. Basic investment information

At some time in our lives most of us have money we do not want to spend immediately. So we save (or invest) it. Whether you are just saving to have a cushion to help out in an emergency or are investing your money to help increase your income, you will be faced with a lot of choices over where to put your money. This chapter will give you some of the basic information you need to help you choose – it will help you think about your finances and sort out your priorities and it explains some of the jargon and terms you will come across. Chapter 15 looks at most of the different investments available and gives details to help you choose what is most suitable for you.

YOUR INVESTMENT STRATEGY

Your personal circumstances and what you want from your money mean that your best choice of investments can be very different from someone else's. But for most people there are four major priorities:

- **An emergency fund.** You never know when you might need a few hundred pounds very quickly. While using credit cards can help in some situations you still may feel more secure if you know that you have £500 or £1,000 which you can get at immediately.

- **A home of your own.** Buying your own home not only ensures you will always have a roof over your head but has proved in the past to be a very worthwhile investment, partly because of the tax advantages – you get tax relief if you borrow to buy (see page 8) and will not have to pay capital gains tax (CGT) on the profit (see below). It is not very easy to cash in your investment in your home but you may be able to move to somewhere smaller or, if you are elderly, you can use the value of your home to provide an income (see page 156).

- **A pension for when you retire**. Don't imagine that the state pension on its own will be enough for you to live comfortably. An employer's pension, if you get one, will help but you still may be glad of extra income when you are older. Tax advantages make investing in pension plans a worthwhile way of saving your money for your retirement (see Chapter 13).

- **Financial protection for your family**. Do you have enough life insurance to help support your family if you were to die young? What would happen if you were unable to work for a long period owing to illness? See Chapter 12 to make sure that your family would be sufficiently well provided for in these events.

Once you have taken care of these basic financial needs you can start thinking about where to put the rest of your money. There are all sorts of things to consider, but they boil down to five main points covering why you are saving; your tax position; the degree of risk you can take; how much money you have got; and your personal circumstances. Why these are important is discussed briefly below; then some of the technical points are explained in more detail.

What do you want from your investments? If you are saving up for a specific event such as next year's holiday or a wedding you will need to look at investments where you can be sure that you can get your money when you want it and where your money will be safe, e.g. a simple building society or bank account. If you want to build up a lump sum to help provide an income in later life you may be able to take more risks with your money as you are looking for long-term growth and are not tied to taking your money out at a particular time.

What is your tax position? Some investments deduct income tax which you can't reclaim if you are a non-taxpayer – so you should look to see if investments which pay interest without deducting tax are a better bet. Elderly people need to think about whether they can avoid losing part (or all) of their age allowance (see page 67) by careful choice of investments. Higher-rate taxpayers might do well by putting their money in tax-free investments or by looking for investments which give mainly a capital gain (which is taxed less highly).

How much risk are you prepared to take? With some investments the number of pounds you have invested cannot fall – but you are unlikely to get spectacular returns. Other investments are more risky – while there may be a chance of making a substantial profit, there is also a chance that the value of your investment could fall – meaning you would get back less than you put in. The way to minimise the risk is to spread your savings between several types of investment to avoid having all your eggs in one basket.

How much money do you have? The larger the amount you have to invest, the greater the spread of investments you will be able to choose. If you don't have much you probably ought not to be thinking about taking risks with any of it. It should be invested mainly in building societies, banks and National Savings, and you could consider putting some of it in index-linked investments to protect it from inflation. But as the years go by, once you have a reasonable amount of money in safe investments you can think about widening your strategy. It would normally be worth putting some of your money into unit trusts, shares, investment trusts and other riskier investments. You can reduce the risk to you by spreading your money between several riskier investments – you're taking a big risk if you put it all in one.

What are your personal circumstances? If you have young children you may want to build up your savings to help with the cost of private schooling. Your investment strategy will be somewhat different from a couple whose children have left home and who are thinking of how best to provide for their retirement. If you know that your income is likely to drop – for instance you are planning to return to college or start a business – you may want to build up your savings to live on. If you want to invest money on a regular basis you will find tailor-made schemes to help you be disciplined in all sorts of different investment fields.

TECHNICAL DETAILS

The money you have to save or invest is often referred to as your 'capital'. Many investments pay you for lending them your capital (in the same way as you pay for borrowing money). Many of these pay in the form of interest – as with a bank or building society account. If this interest is paid out to you as income, your capital will not increase, and you will get back the same number of pounds as you invested in the first place.

Other investments do not pay interest in return for you lending them money; instead they pay you by giving you more back when you want your investment out than you put in – as with National Savings Certificates. So instead of getting an income from your investment you get capital growth.

Some investments combine both these sorts of return. For instance, if you buy shares you will receive a share in the company's profits, normally every six months – so you get a regular income. And you also hope that the price of your shares will increase so you can sell them for more than you paid – so you get capital growth too.

You can turn most interest-paying investments into capital-growth ones quite easily – simply leave the interest in your account so it is added to your capital and itself earns interest. The amount of capital you have then increases steadily.

Risk

Investments are always a gamble, and you can never be absolutely certain that you have picked the one that will make the most money. But although you can't do anything about that risk you should be aware of the three other main risks you take when investing.

Can the number of pounds you have invested fall? With some investments you might *lose* money, not make it. For instance, if you invest in shares or unit trusts the value of your investment will fluctuate almost daily depending on what profits the various companies make, what is happening to interest rates, what is happening in the economy both here and abroad, and so on. So the time you both buy and sell is important – ideally you want to buy when prices are low and sell when they are high. If you get it right you can make large profits but if you get it wrong you could lose a lot of money.

The first rule in dealing with this sort of risk is that you should not invest any money you can't afford to lose or that you might need back in a hurry (for you might have to sell at a time when prices are much lower than when you bought). The second rule is that you should spread your money around, not put it into a single risky investment. The chances of a number of investments all doing badly are much lower than the chance of one being a disastrous choice. (However, in the same way you also reduce your chance of doing very well.)

How safe is your money? Some institutions are safer than others and have more regulations governing their operations. For example, there is little chance of the Government not repaying money you have invested in British Government Stock or National Savings. But investing in companies which operate outside Britain (even if it is only in the Channel Islands) can be much more risky as there are not the same safeguards for investors and restrictions on what companies can and can't do as there are in the United Kingdom. And investing in small, new companies is likely to be a riskier business than buying shares in a large, well-established and well-known company.

What about inflation? Inflation is all about rising prices and if you want your capital to be able to buy the same amount in ten years as it does now it will have to rise along with inflation. So if prices in general rise by 5% a year, the value of your investment has to rise by the same amount just to keep up with inflation. Anything you get over the rate of inflation is called the 'real return'. Over the last few years inflation has been 5% or less and it has been relatively easy to find returns of 8% or 9% (or even higher) and so get a real return of 3% or more.

But this hasn't always been the case – in the 1970s inflation tended to be much higher than the return on investments so that the value of your capital in terms of what you could buy with it dropped steadily. The only sure way of insuring against this is by investing in index-linked investments where the value of your capital increases with inflation.

Tax considerations

Any money you make as a result of investing your capital is likely to be taxable. If your investment pays out interest or income at regular intervals the tax involved will be income tax, while if the investment is the sort where you buy something and hope to sell it at a profit, it will be capital gains tax.

Income Tax

Any investment is likely to be in one of four groups:

- **Tax-free**, e.g. National Savings Certificates, National Savings Yearly Plan, Personal Equity Plans. No matter how much other income you have you will not have to pay any tax on your interest.
- **Tax-paid, non-refundable**, e.g. bank and building society accounts, local authority loans. When you receive your interest, it has had the equivalent of basic-rate tax already deducted. If your income is high, you may have to pay extra tax on the interest but if your income is not high enough for you to have to pay tax you cannot reclaim the tax that has been paid on your behalf.
- **Tax-paid, refundable**, e.g. dividends from shares or unit trusts. When you receive your interest or dividend it has had basic-rate tax deducted. You may owe extra tax if you have a high income, but if your income is not high enough for you to have to pay tax you can reclaim the tax that has been deducted.
- **Gross-paid**, e.g. National Savings Income Bonds. You get the interest paid in full, without any tax having been deducted. If your income is not high enough for you to have to pay any tax you can keep all the interest. If you are a taxpayer you will owe tax on the amount of the interest.

Capital gains tax

Capital gains tax (CGT) is a way of taxing money you make out of selling things at a profit. About the only conventional investments that you might have to pay CGT on are shares and unit trusts – but for completeness, this section explains the basic CGT rules and how they can affect any profit you make. First, though, there are some things that you don't ever have to pay CGT on:

- Your only or main home.
- Private cars.
- Personal belongings worth £3,000 or less each when you sell them.
- Personal belongings with an expected life of less than 50 years.
- National Savings Certificates, Yearly Plan, Premium Bonds.
- Proceeds from life insurance.

- British Government Stock.
- Collections of British money.

This is quite a wide-ranging list of exemptions so you can see that there isn't that much that ordinary people might find themselves having to pay CGT on. The most likely things apart from shares and unit trusts are a second home or land, and your business. Working out whether there is any CGT due on items (or 'assets') which *are* taxable is quite complicated. But it's worth saying first of all that there will be no tax at all to pay if the profits you have made on all the things you have sold or given away in a single tax year come to less than a certain amount, which in 1987–88 is £6,600.

Then, not covered here, special rules apply if you are selling or retiring from running a business. And if you give something away which would be liable for tax, you and the person receiving the gift can agree to put off paying the tax until the recipient parts with the gifts – called 'roll-over relief'.

You can't escape the tax by getting rid of assets on the cheap – if you give things away or sell them cut-price you will be taxed as if you had sold them at their full market value.

The first step in working out whether you have to pay any CGT is to find the final value of each of the assets you don't have at the end of the tax year that you did have at the beginning. For shares or unit trusts this will be the price at which you sold them.

Then deduct the initial value, i.e. the price you paid or the market value at the time you acquired the asset. But because a large part of the gain you make can be due to inflation, for things you have acquired since March 1982 you can increase the price paid (or market value) by the rate of inflation since you acquired it. (Different rules apply for things acquired before March 1982.) You can also add on to the initial value certain expenses involved in getting or disposing of the asset such as advertising costs, legal fees, etc. and anything you have spent to increase its value (apart from ordinary maintenance).

When you subtract the initial value for each item from its final value, the figure for each asset will either be a plus figure, in which case you have made a gain, or a negative figure where you have made a loss. The final step in working out your CGT bill is to add up all the gains and deduct the losses. If the total is more than a certain amount (£6,600 in the 1987–88 tax year) you have to pay tax at 30% on the excess. If the total is less than this, there's no tax to pay. A married couple get only this much between them (unless they are separated). If you think you have CGT to pay, make sure you have included all your losses. Because of the inflation-proofing rules, you may have made a 'loss' when you got rid of an asset without realising it. For example, building society investments count as assets (with most accounts you are technically buying a share in the building society) and because of inflation you will always make a loss in CGT terms when you cash-in your investment, i.e. close your account. It is also important to plan when you sell and buy assets to make the most of your tax-free limit – if you don't use it up in one year, you cannot carry it over to the next.

More information

CGT8 Capital gains tax
CGT11 Capital gains tax and the small businessman
CGT12 Capital gains tax: Indexation
(All available from your local tax office)

Comparing investments

If you are choosing between investments, you need to be able to compare what you are going to get in the way of interest or capital growth. What you have to find out is the yearly rate of return on your capital.

If an investment pays out interest, and interest only, the rate of return depends on how often the interest is paid out. For example, if you invest £100 in an account paying interest of 10% a year, then after one year you will get £10 interest and at the end of the year you will have £110. But if instead the interest was paid in two instalments of 5% every six months, after the first six months you would get £5 interest and the balance in your account would be £105. After the remaining six months you would get the second instalment of 5% paid on the £105 which would be £5.25 so that your balance at the end of year would be £110.25. This gives a yearly return of 10.25%. The more frequently interest is paid or added to the account the higher will be the yearly return (see Table 4).

Table 4   True interest rates.

Quoted rate	True rate if interest paid			
%	yearly %	half-yearly %	quarterly %	monthly %
6.5	6.5	6.6	6.65	6.7
7.0	7.0	7.1	7.2	7.25
7.5	7.5	7.65	7.7	7.75
8.0	8.0	8.15	8.25	8.3
8.5	8.5	8.7	8.75	8.85
9.0	9.0	9.2	9.3	9.4
9.5	9.5	9.75	9.85	9.9
10.0	10.0	10.25	10.4	10.45
10.5	10.5	10.8	10.9	11.0
11.0	11.0	11.3	11.45	11.55

With capital-growth investments, it is still possible to calculate a yearly rate of return so that you can compare them with interest-type investments. Many companies will do this in their advertisements or investment literature. Table 5 might give you an idea of what sort of return you're getting.

Table 5   Equivalent interest rates for capital growth.

At end of year	Equivalent interest rate if £1,000 has grown to						
	£1,100	£1,200	£1,500	£1,750	£2,000	£2,500	£3,000
	%	%	%	%	%	%	%
2	4.9	9.5	22.5				
3	3.2	6.3	14.5	20.5	26.0		
4	2.4	4.7	10.7	15.0	18.9	25.7	
5	1.9	3.7	8.5	11.8	14.9	20.1	24.6
10	1.0	1.8	4.1	5.8	7.2	9.6	11.6

Even when you are sure you are looking at real rates of return, there are three other points to consider before you can be sure you are comparing like with like:

■ Is the return fixed or can it vary? Many bank and building society accounts will change the interest they pay as interest rates in general rise and fall. But the return on National Savings Certificates is fixed, so that when you buy them you know exactly what you will get out in five years' time.

- What about tax? Check whether the return quoted is 'gross' (i.e. what you get before any tax is paid) or 'net' (what you get after tax has been paid).
- What is the quoted return based on? With speculative investments, such as unit trusts and shares, the return will be either a guess as to what you might get, or a carefully-chosen look at what happened in the past. Neither is any guide to what you will actually get.

GETTING ADVICE

There is no shortage of people wanting to give you investment advice; the problem is that they will all give different advice. And few are genuinely independent, as many will get a commission for recommending a particular savings institution. Before seeking advice from anyone you should use the guidelines in this chapter to get an idea of what it is you want from your money. You could also look at a few of the many money magazines now available; *Which?* magazine is often a very good general guide and is completely independent of all the financial institutions so is able to give completely unbiased general advice. Your local library may have copies.

All sorts of people give financial advice – newspapers, bank managers, solicitors, accountants and so on. The more an adviser asks about your personal circumstances, the better. You should be asked for details of your family, your home, income, tax position, financial commitments, pension rights, what you want from your investments, what risk you are prepared to take, what savings you already have, your plans for the future and so on. A good adviser should also explain why he/she is recommending certain investments for you and answer any questions you ask. It won't do any harm to get a second opinion – and whatever you do, don't be forced into investing in something you are unhappy about.

15. A bird's-eye view of investments

In this chapter you will find an alphabetical list of many of the main types of investment with brief details of how they work and the tax position. The alphabetical list makes it easy to look up a particular investment. The lists below groups investments according to whether they are suitable for various purposes.

No risk to your capital and fixed returns

Banks (fixed term, fixed rate deposit accounts)
Building society fixed rate bonds
British Government Stock
Income and growth bonds
Local authority loans
National Savings Certificates
National Savings Yearly Plan

No risk to your capital but variable returns

Banks
Building societies
National Savings Investment Account
National Savings Income or Deposit Bonds

Inflation-proofed savings and/or income

Index-linked investments

For non-taxpayers

British Government Stock
National Savings investments

For capital growth but with risk

Business Expansion Scheme
British Government Stock
Investment trusts
Personal Equity Plans
Shares
Unit trusts

For regular, monthly income

Banks
Building societies
National Savings Income Bonds
Unit trusts

For regular income for older people

Annuities
Income bonds

For regular savings

Banks
Building societies
National Savings Yearly Plan
Unit trusts

Annuities

You pay an insurance company a lump sum, and it pays you a regular income in return until you die. The income you get depends on the following:

- **Your age.** The older you are when you buy the annuity, the higher the income you get because the chances are that you will die sooner than a younger person.
- **Your sex.** A woman will get a smaller income than a man of the same age as on average women live longer than men.
- **Interest rates.** The income you get is fixed at the time you buy the annuity and the higher interest rates are, the higher will be your income.

There are several types of annuity. The simplest pay out a

fixed income only until you die and the capital you invested is not returnable under any circumstances. Joint life annuities pay income to a couple until they are both dead. With an increasing annuity the income rises each year, either by a set amount or along with inflation, though the initial level is much less than with a fixed payment. Some annuities will guarantee to pay out for, say, five years even if you die earlier; others will repay to your heirs the difference between what you invested and what you have received – again the level of payment will be lower than a simple annuity.

Home income plans are a way of releasing capital locked-up in your home to provide an income. An insurance company gives you a mortgage secured on your home and the money is used to buy an annuity. Some of this is used to pay the interest on the loan; the rest is yours to spend. The original loan is repaid out of your estate when you die, normally by selling your home.

Tax

Not all the income you receive from an annuity is taxable as part of it is treated as being a return of your original investment, the amount depending on your sex and age. The older you are, the greater the proportion of the income that is tax-free.

Verdict

Annuities are suitable really only for people over 65 who need an income; and the older you are the better.

Banks

Banks offer a variety of savings accounts in which you invest your capital and get paid interest. In general, the larger the amount of money you have to invest and the longer the notice you are prepared to give, the higher the interest paid. The simplest accounts pay a variable interest rate depending on interest rates in general, and some allow you to have your money out immediately; others ask for a fixed period of notice such as one week or one month, or more. The interest may be paid out to you or it may be left in the account to add to your capital.

Some banks offer chequebook facilities on a savings account, though you should look at the conditions carefully and make sure they are suitable for you. You may also find accounts designed for people who want to save regular amounts – watch out for the conditions, particularly on whether you can miss any payments and how many withdrawals you can make without penalty. Banks also offer fixed interest rate, fixed term investments where you can choose how long you want to invest your capital – anything from short periods such as a month, to six months or a year. The rates on offer will vary almost daily.

Tax

All bank accounts pay their interest after deducting the equivalent of basic-rate tax. Non-taxpayers can't reclaim this interest; higher-rate taxpayers will owe more tax.

Verdict

In a bank account there is no risk of your losing your capital (though inflation can erode its value). You could consider a bank account as a suitable home for your emergency savings or for savings which you want kept safe. And you could look at a bank high interest cheque account to replace a current account which doesn't pay interest. But you should shop around between banks and also look at what is on offer from the building societies.

British Government Stock

Often known as 'gilt-edged securities' or just 'gilts', British Government Stock is one way in which the Government raises money for its spending plans. In return for lending the Government money, you get interest. 'Treasury 11¾% 1996' seems a rather long-winded name but it tells you that 1996 is the redemption date (when the Government will repay the loan); 11¾% (the 'coupon') means that until that date the Government will pay you that much interest on the face value of the stock, usually in two instalments a year. Index-linked gilts are also available (see below).

Gilts are traded on The Stock Exchange (so you can buy them through a stockbroker) and the price at which a stock is sold will vary from day to day. You may pay only £80 for £100 face value of stock or you may pay £110. It all depends on what is happening in the financial markets at the time (and what people think is going to happen in the future).

You can look at British Government Stock in two ways. If you invest and hold on until the redemption date you will know exactly what your return will be over that period – it could be a combination of income and a capital gain (if you buy the stock at less than its face value) or income and a capital loss (if you buy the stock at higher than its face value). Many daily papers carry details of the price of stocks traded the previous day and include the return you would get if you held the stock until redemption. But you can also buy and sell stocks like shares hoping to make a quick profit. A stockbroker will be able to advise you on which stocks are most suitable for you.

Tax

The income you get from Government stocks is taxable and is usually paid out after deduction of basic-rate tax, which you can reclaim if you are not a taxpayer. Higher-rate taxpayers will owe extra tax. If you buy gilts through the National Savings Stock Register at a post office the income will be paid out without deducting tax – a particularly useful facility if you are a non-taxpayer. (But it can be a more expensive way of buying a large investment than dealing with a broker.) If you make a capital gain, either when you sell stock or if you hold it until the redemption date, your gain will be exempt from capital gains tax.

Verdict

Government stock is a safe investment if you keep it until the redemption date, as you know exactly how much you will get back. If you buy and sell in the hope of making quick gains you could lose if you mis-read the market and buy or sell at the wrong time, as the best time to buy is when interest rates are high but gilt prices are low. Then as interest rates fall, the prices will rise. If you are a higher-rate taxpayer or over 64 and in the age allowance trap (see page 67), you should consider choosing stocks with a low interest rate so that most of the return you get will be a non-taxable capital gain.

Building societies

Building society accounts are very similar to bank accounts – your capital is safe and you get paid interest. You will find a variety of different accounts with minimum investments ranging from £1 to £20,000 or even more, notice of withdrawal varying from none up to three or six months, and a variety of interest rates and other conditions. Almost all building society accounts offer variable interest, though occasionally (particularly if interest rates are due to rise) there will be one or two fixed-rate bonds on offer. Several building societies have cheque accounts – as with banks you should check the conditions and rules carefully before deciding on one. Regular savings accounts are available at many building societies.

Tax

All building society accounts pay interest after deduction of the equivalent of basic-rate tax. Non-taxpayers can't reclaim this tax; higher-rate taxpayers will owe extra tax.   .

Verdict

There is no risk of losing your capital in a building society account (though inflation will reduce its value). A building society account could be a suitable home for your emergency fund or for money where you want your capital to be protected. You could consider a building society cheque account as an alternative to a bank current account. Never be tempted to invest money in an account which requires notice for withdrawals if there is a good chance you will need the money more quickly, as if you withdraw without giving the appropriate notice you will lose interest. Before investing shop around to get the best rates.

More information

Building Society Choice, (available from Riverside House, Rattlesden, Bury St Edmunds, Suffolk IP30 0SF) provides up-to-date information on investment rates through an independent monthly magazine

Business Expansion Scheme

To encourage investment in the shares of certain companies (usually small new businesses which are not quoted on The Stock Exchange or the Unlisted Securities Market) the Business Expansion Scheme (BES) allows tax relief at your top rate of tax on investments of up to £40,000 each year. In order to get the full tax advantages you normally have to keep the shares for five years. There are two ways of investing: directly, in which case you have to buy at least £500 of shares in each company, or through an Inland Revenue approved fund in which you must invest at least £2,000. If your top rate of tax is 50% and you invest £5,000 then the investment will cost you only £2,500. If when you sell in five years' time you get back the full £5,000, the return to you will be the equivalent of 15% a year, tax-free. But of course, you take the risk that you will lose some (or even all) of your investment.

Tax

As well as getting full tax relief at your highest rate of tax on your investment, any gain you make when you sell shares bought later than 18 March 1986 will be free of Capital Gains Tax. (Non-taxpayers, of course, get no benefit from BES relief.)

Verdict

Investing in BES is risky – that's why there are so many tax advantages. According to statistics, around one in six of the companies which you could invest in via BES in the first two years of its operation failed. So it is really for you only if you are a higher-rate taxpayer with spare money that you are prepared to gamble away. You must also be prepared to leave your investment alone for at least five years – if you sell your shares earlier you will lose some or all of your tax relief. If you are interested, visit several advisers to see what they recommend and study any literature very carefully. Pay particular attention to charges.

More information

IR51 The business expansion scheme
(Available from your local tax office)

BES Magazine
(Available from 25 Bedford Row, London WC1R 4HE)
BES Investment Newsletter
(Available from 100 Fleet Street, London EC4Y 1DE)
Investors Chronicle
(Available from your local newsagent or library)

Income and growth bonds

Both of these are insurance company investments where you hand over a lump sum and get a guaranteed return on your capital for a fixed number of years – commonly five or ten. An income bond pays the return as income, usually once or twice a year, while a growth bond re-invests the money in the bond to build up a larger sum for when the bond comes to the end of its term.

Technically bonds can be quite complicated and often are a combination of investment-type life insurance policies and annuities. The type of bond can be quite important if you are a higher-rate taxpayer or are elderly as some may be a better buy than others.

Tax

The way you pay tax (and how much you pay) will also vary depending on the particular bond you buy. But in general the return on bonds is paid after deduction of basic-rate tax. Non-taxpayers can reclaim this tax with some kinds of bonds, though not all – so make sure you check with the company before buying. Higher-rate taxpayers will usually owe extra tax.

Verdict

If you have a lump sum to invest (usually at least £1,000) and do not mind being unable to get at it for some time it may be worth looking at income and growth bonds. And as the return is fixed at the outset you can be certain of your income and also, perhaps, be able to lock into high interest rates before they fall. Certain types of bond are particularly suitable for elderly people. But you could also consider National Savings Certificates, British Government Stocks held to redemption, or local authority loans. Typically, a bond will be on the market for only a relatively short period of time. A broker should be able to advise you on what bonds are available – if you are not a basic-rate taxpayer make sure you get quotes for what your after-tax return will be before deciding on a bond.

Index-linked investments

It is really only the Government that is able to afford to guarantee to keep your savings up with inflation. Index-linked British Government Stocks work in a similar way to ordinary gilts but the income you receive and the face value of the stock you buy is increased in line with inflation. With index-linked National Savings Certificates the amount you invest is increased each year in line with inflation and you get interest each year based on the revalued amount. So you are guaranteed to get a fixed real return, i.e. a return so much above inflation. National Savings Indexed Income Bonds pay a monthly income which is guaranteed to rise in line with inflation. But the capital you invest is not increased – so if you invest £5,000 you will get back only £5,000.

Tax

This is the same as for the equivalent non-indexed products.

Verdict

Whether you should put some of your savings into index-linked investments really depends on what you think is going to happen both to inflation and to interest rates. For the last few years inflation has been relatively low and interest rates high so investing in index-linked investments would have meant that you missed out on the much higher returns available from ordinary investments. But when inflation is high (as it was during the 1970s), index-linked products may well be among the highest-paying investments.

More information

Leaflets are available from main post offices

Investment trusts

If you put money into an investment trust you are buying shares in an investment company quoted on The Stock Exchange. Their business is to make money by investing in shares of other companies, property and so on. Share-holders can vote at meetings and are paid a share of the company's profits in the form of a dividend just as if they had bought a share in a manufacturing or retail company.

The price you pay for shares does not depend directly on the value of what assets the investment trust holds but on how many other people want to buy the trust's shares and how many want to sell.

Tax

Basic-rate tax is deducted from dividends before they are paid to share-holders. Non-taxpayers can reclaim this tax; higher-rate taxpayers will owe extra tax. If you sell your shares and make a profit you may have to pay capital gains tax.

Verdict

If you want to invest in a wide range of shares, one way is to do it indirectly through an investment trust. This will be cheaper than trying to buy a well-balanced selection of shares by yourself. But all investments which involve stocks and shares are risky in that the value of your capital is not protected and if you needed your money out in a hurry you could find that you came out with less than you invested. So don't consider investing money you cannot afford to lose in investment trusts.

More information

Association of Investment Trust Companies (Park House, 16 Finsbury Circus, London EC2M 7JJ)
Investment Trust Yearbook (Available in large public libraries)

Local authority loans

With a local authority loan (or bond) you lend money to a local authority for a fixed number of years – anything from one to ten, and in return you get interest at a rate fixed at the outset.

Tax

Interest is usually paid out twice a year with the equivalent of basic-rate tax already deducted. Non-taxpayers can't claim this tax; higher-rate taxpayers will owe more.

Verdict

Local authority loans can be useful if you want a fixed return and a guarantee that you will get your capital back. If interest rates are about to fall it can be a useful way of making sure your interest remains at the old, high rates. But you will be locking your money away for some years so be sure that you will not want it earlier.

More information

CIPFA Loans Bureau
(Tel. 01-638 6361 between 3.30 and 5 pm for up-to-date rates)

National Savings

The Government gets some of the money it needs for its spending plans by selling National Savings investments. You invest in National Savings at a post office.

An Ordinary Account is a deposit account from which you can withdraw money immediately without having to give notice. The first £70 of interest you get each year is tax-free (£140 for a married couple) but the relatively low interest rate reduces this advantage somewhat.

An Investment Account needs one month's notice if you want to withdraw any of your savings. Interest is added to the account on 31 December each year. If you are a non-taxpayer, the return is likely to be higher than you could get from a building society or bank; taxpayers should check the rates available elsewhere – remember to compare either after-tax rates or before-tax rates.

Deposit Bonds require three month's notice if you want to make a withdrawal and if you take money out within a year of investing it you lose interest on it. Interest is added to your bond after you have had your money invested for a year, and on the same date in following years. Income Bonds are similar but the interest is paid monthly. If you are a taxpayer compare rates and investment conditions available elsewhere – you may be able to get the same (or a higher) rate without having to tie your money up for so long.

Savings Certificates offer a guaranteed tax-free return on money invested for at least a year. Interest is added at the end of the first year, then every three months at a rate which increases each year. You can get a regular income by cashing-in certificates each year after the first. Because the return is tax-free, National Savings Certificates are particularly attractive to higher-rate taxpayers.

The Yearly Plan for regular monthly savings guarantees a fixed tax-free return if you save for a year and then leave your savings alone for up to five years.

Tax

All National Savings investments which pay out income pay it out without deducting tax so that they are particularly suitable for non-taxpayers. Taxpayers will owe tax except with National Savings Certificates which are tax-free – so are an increasingly attractive proposition the higher your top rate of tax.

Personal Equity Plans

Personal Equity Plans (PEPs) are designed to encourage first-time share-holders. You can invest up to £2,400 a year in shares through an Inland Revenue authorised plan manager, and receive the dividends and any profits free of income and capital gains taxes. To get these advantages you have to keep your money in the PEP until at least the end of the year following the year in which you invested. Each year you can invest in only one PEP, even if you invest less than the maximum, but you can choose a different plan each year.

Tax

The returns from PEPs are completely free of taxes.

Verdict

Though the money you invest will be pooled with lots of other savers, your PEP is unlikely to invest in more than say three shares – which isn't really a wide enough spread to reduce your risks very much. Charges made by plan managers vary widely and can be very high – they could easily wipe out any savings you make by not having to pay tax. Non-taxpayers will receive no advantage – they can already reclaim the tax paid on dividends. Higher-rate taxpayers and those already paying capital gains tax will benefit most from PEPs, but the amounts they can invest are relatively small so they won't have a lot of effect on tax bills.

More information

Good PEP Guide (Available from Riverside House, Rattlesden, Bury St Edmunds, Suffolk IP30 0SF) is an independent magazine giving comparative information on PEP charges
Personal Equity Plans, John Campbell (Woodhead-Faulkner)

Shares

If you buy shares in a company you are effectively helping to finance that company and in return get a share of the company's profits in the form of a 'dividend'. The price of shares will vary from day to day (even from minute to minute) depending on the balance of potential buyers and sellers which in turn will depend on such things as how well the company is doing, what the prospects in that part of industry are, what is happening in the world economy and so on. A company which meets certain conditions is allowed to have its shares listed on The Stock Exchange; the shares of newer, more speculative companies may be bought and sold in a different market-place such as the Unlisted Securities Market.

You can buy and sell shares through a stockbroker, your accountant, at banks and even at a few building societies. They all make charges of one sort or another and these charges generally mean that it is not worth buying less than £750 to £1,000 worth of shares in a company. But investing in just one company can be risky – the price could plummet as soon as you have bought – so you should aim to invest in at least ten or so companies operating in different industries and services so as to spread your risk. (Of course, by doing this you also lessen the chance of making huge gains by having invested all your money in one company whose shares suddenly rocket in value.)

Tax

Dividends are paid after basic-rate tax has been deducted. Non-taxpayers can reclaim this; higher-rate taxpayers will owe extra. If you make a profit when you sell shares you may have to pay capital gains tax.

Verdict

Shares are for people who are prepared to risk their money in the hope of making a large return. If you haven't enough money to build up a balanced 'portfolio' quickly or if you might need the money quickly (when share prices could be low) or if the thought of your capital going up and down in value with share prices worries you – don't invest in shares.

More information

Various booklets are available from the Public Affairs Office, The Stock Exchange, London EC2N 1HP
The Share-owner's Guide, J. T. Stafford (Woodhead-Faulkner)

Unit trusts

When you buy units in a unit trust your money is pooled with that of lots of other investors and the total used to buy shares or British Government Stocks. The unit trust company makes the decisions about what to invest in and when to buy and sell. Each particular unit trust will invest in certain types of investments – there are general unit trusts which invest in a wide variety of shares and gilts, specialist funds which invest in one particular sort of industry such as energy or in one geographical area such as the Far East or Australia.

The main advantage of investing via a unit trust is that you can invest in a wide variety of shares with a relatively small investment – as little as £200, or even £20 a month. Even so, for real safety you should invest in several different trusts. There is no guarantee that a trust which has done well in the past will continue to do so in the future, and spreading your investment across several will help reduce your risk still further.

The price you pay depends on the value of investments in the fund and there is no commission to pay as the costs are taken care of in the difference between the price at which you buy (the 'offer' price) and that at which you sell (the 'bid' price). Once you have bought into a unit trust the value of your units will fluctuate along with the value of the investments in the fund. Unit trusts make a management charge each year – typically ¾% or 1% of the value of your investment.

Unit trusts usually pay out income twice a year although a few pay out monthly, If you want monthly income it is also possible to put together a 'portfolio' of unit trusts where one pays out each month.

Tax

Basic-rate tax will have been deducted before you get income from a unit trust and non-taxpayers can reclaim this. Higher-rate taxpayers will owe extra tax. Even if the income is re-invested in the unit trust instead of being paid out it will have tax deducted in the same way. If you make a profit when you sell your units you may have to pay capital gains tax.

Verdict

Unit trusts are for people who like the idea of taking the risk of investing in stocks and shares but perhaps don't have enough money to invest directly and get a well-balanced holding of different shares. Or perhaps for people who don't want the bother of forever checking on their investments and making buying and selling decisions. If you can't afford to take risks with your money or might need it in an emergency and be forced to sell even if prices are low, don't invest in unit trusts. And you should be prepared to treat them as long-term investments.

More information

Everything you need to know about unit trusts
(Available from Booklet Department, Unit Trust Association, Park House, 16 Finsbury Circus, London EC2M 7JP)
Unit Trusts, Sara Williams (Woodhead-Faulkner)

List of acronyms

APR	annual percentage rate of interest
ATM	automated teller machine
AVC	additional voluntary contribution
BES	Business Expansion Scheme
CAB	Citizens Advice Bureau
CGT	capital gains tax
DHSS	Department of Health and Social Security
FIS	family income supplement
GMP	guaranteed minimum pension
LEA	local education authority
MIRAS	mortgage interest relief at source
NHS	National Health Service
OPAS	Occupational Pensions Advisory Service
PAYE	Pay As You Earn
PEP	Personal Equity Plan
SDA	severe disablement allowance
SERPS	State Earnings Related Pension Scheme
SMP	statutory maternity pay
SSP	statutory sick pay
VAT	value added tax

Index

THE WOODHEAD-FAULKNER MONEYGUIDES

The Share-owner's Guide: How to invest
profitably and safely in shares

J. T. Stafford

Family Finance: How to make your money
go further

Sue Thomas

The Home-owner's Guide: Buying, building,
improving and running your own home

Judith Hargreaves

Personal Equity Plans: How to build up a
nest egg – with tax relief

John Campbell

Unit Trusts

Sara Williams